YOUR MONEY LIFE: YOUR 40s

Peter Dunn

Cengage Learning PTR

Australia, ted States

CENGAGE
Learning®

Professional • Technical • Reference

Your Money Life:
Your 40s
Peter Dunn

Publisher and General
Manager, Cengage
Learning PTR:
Stacy L. Hiquet

Associate Director
of Marketing:
Sarah Panella

Manager of Editorial
Services:
Heather Talbot

Senior Product
Manager:
Mitzi Koontz

Project Editor/
Copy Editor:
Cathleen D. Small

Interior Layout Tech:
Bill Hartman

Indexer:
Sharon Shock

Proofreader:
Gene Redding

For product information and technology assistance, contact us at
Cengage Learning Customer & Sales Support, 1-800-354-9706

For permission to use material from this text or product,
submit all requests online at **cengage.com/permissions**
Further permissions questions can be emailed to
permissionrequest@cengage.com

All trademarks are the property of their respective owners.

All images © Peter Dunn unless otherwise noted.

Library of Congress Control Number: 2014954401

ISBN-13: 978-1-305-50796-8

ISBN-10: 1-305-50796-7

Cengage Learning PTR
20 Channel Center Street
Boston, MA 02210
USA

Cengage Learning is a leading provider of customized learning solutions
with office locations around the globe, including Singapore, the United
Kingdom, Australia, Mexico, Brazil, and Japan. Locate your local office at:
international.cengage.com/region

Cengage Learning products are represented in Canada by
Nelson Education, Ltd.

For your lifelong learning solutions, visit **cengageptr.com**

Visit our corporate website at **cengage.com**

Printed in the United States of America
1 2 3 4 5 6 7 16 15 14

This book is dedicated to you, the reader. The words in this book aren't about me or my family or anyone else who may have inspired me at some point in my life. This book is about you and Your Money Life. *May the words impact and serve you.*

ABOUT THE AUTHOR

Peter Dunn is an author, radio host, and personal finance expert who has developed content and curriculum for some of the world's largest financial companies. He was a financial advisor for nearly 15 years and managed several millions of dollars in assets. He is known for his down-to-earth and humorous approach that resonates with both consumers and financial industry insiders. He appears regularly on Fox News, Fox Business, and CNN Headline News, as well as several nationally syndicated radio programs. In 2012, Cision named him the fourth most influential personal finance broadcaster in the nation. Today, Peter's financial wellness firm develops financial wellness curricula for Fortune 500 companies.

Learn more at PeteThePlanner.com.

CONTENTS

Chapter 1: The Path   1

You're in a Sandwich   3
What You Will Learn   7
    Debt   7
    Spending   8
    Budgeting   8
    Major Purchases   9
    Credit   9
    Saving and Investing   10
    Insurance   10
A Plan   11
Your Removable Guide   11
Get Started   12

Chapter 2: The Past: Debt   13

The Cheap-Money Fallacy   15
Types of Debt   17
    Student Loans   18
    Parent Student Loans   20
    Bank Credit Card Debt   22
    Store Credit Card Debt   24
    Car Loan   25
    Home Loan (Mortgage)   26
    Medical Debt   27
    Lines of Credit (Secured and Unsecured)   28
    401(k) Loans   30

Personal Loans (from a Financial Institution)	31
Personal Loans (from a Family Member or Friend)	32
Tax Debt	33
Collection Debt	33
Judgments	34
A Closer Look at Debt and Paying It Down	36
Your Relationship with Debt	37
Debt Pay-Down Process	38
The Math Method	39
The Momentum Method	41
The Shotgun Method	41
Getting Out of Debt	42
Step 1: Map Out Your Debt	43
Step 2: Build Momentum with Small Debt Victories	43
Step 3: Commit to a Debt-Payment Schedule	46
Your Perspective Needs to Shift	47
What Now?	48

Chapter 3: The Present: Spending   49

How Using a Credit Card Complicates Spending	53
If Not a Credit Card, Then What?	58
Should You Select Debit or Credit When Swiping Your Debit Card?	61
How Do You Actually Reduce Spending?	63
Groceries	64
Dining Out	66
Utilities	67
The New Necessities	70
Is It Ever Okay to Splurge?	73

Chapter 4: The Pie: Budgeting 75

Is It Time to Relent? 79
The Ideal Household Budget 80
    Rent/Mortgage, Including Property Taxes and
        Property Insurance: 25 Percent 82
    Transportation: 15 Percent 83
    Groceries and Dining Out: 12 Percent 85
    Savings: 10 Percent 87
    Utilities: 10 Percent 88
    Charity: 5 Percent 89
    Clothing: 5 Percent 90
    Medical: 5 Percent 91
    Entertainment: 5 Percent 91
    Holidays and Gifts: 5 Percent 92
    Miscellaneous: 3 Percent 92
The Expense Categories You Don't See 93
    Student Loans 93
    Education 94
    Debt Reduction 95
    Vacation 95
    Kids 96
But I Do All My Shopping at One Store 97
How Do Your Expenses Stack Up? 99

Chapter 5: The Possessions: Major Purchases 101

Housing 102
    Your Monthly Commitment 103
    Five Signs That You Bought Too Much House 105
    The Key to Housing Success 109
    The Importance of a Good Realtor 112
    Home Improvements 114
    What Really Adds Value to Your Home 116

Car	119
But Really, Should You Buy or Lease a New Car?	121
Your Next Car Purchase	124
College Education	127
The Final Factor in Making Big Purchases	132

Chapter 6: The Picture: Credit   133

How Do I Find Out Where I Stand with Creditors?	138
What to Look for on Your Credit Report	139
Repair and Build Your Credit	141
What Your Credit Score Means	143
Is It Really Fixed?	144
What Credit Scores and Dieting Have in Common	145
Three Steps to Improving Bad Credit (or to Maintaining Good Credit)	146
How Your Score Is Calculated	148
Your Kids' Credit	150
What If Your Kids Have No Credit at All?	153
Beyond Credit	156

Chapter 7: The Piggy Bank: Saving and Investing   157

The Role of Net Worth as a Wealth-Building Tool	159
The Three Buckets	163
Bucket #3	164
Bucket #1	165
Bucket #2	167
Types of Investments and Investment Vehicles	168
Stock	169
Bond	170
Mutual Fund	170
Exchange Traded Fund	171

Index Fund 172
Target-Date Fund 172
IRA 174
Roth IRA 174
401(k) 175
529 College Savings Plan 175
Annuity 176
Why You Can't Wait to Invest 179
One More Note on the Match 181
Saving for College 187
Hiring a Financial Advisor 188
Fees for a Financial Advisor 193
Evaluating Your Financial Advisor 195
Risk 200
Dealing with Reality 203

Chapter 8: The Pitfalls: Insurance 205

Consider Getting an Insurance Agent 207
Types of Insurance 208
Health 208
Car 210
Renters 213
Homeowners 214
Life 215
Disability 225
Review Your Coverage Annually 228

Chapter 9: The Plan   229

Choose Your Own Adventure   232
    Questions   232
    Plans   234
Extreme Solutions   238
    Get an Additional Job   239
    Sell Your House   241
Your Diligence and Discipline Will Pay Dividends   244

Index   245

CHAPTER 1

THE PATH

Lordy, lordy, look who bought this book. There is no decade in your financial life as potentially diverse as your forties. For different people, forties can mean anything from retirement, to buying a first home, to becoming a grandparent, to getting married, to getting divorced, and to getting married all over again. All the while, you're heading toward your prime earning years. Your forties is also your last chance to right your ship by choice. If your financial ship is sailing in the wrong direction in your fifties, either you will be forced to change or you will suffer financially for the remainder of your life.

I know, I know, that's pretty severe. But it's true. You've shaken the financial childishness out of yourself, you've laid down some roots, and you are supposed to be setting the tone for the rest of your financial life. It's exciting! And it can be quite terrifying.

In a perfect world, you'd have your house paid off by age 45, and you'd glide into retirement with very few financial obligations and a vast majority of your income committed to retirement savings on a monthly basis. If I just described your life, great job. If I just described a scenario that seems as foreign to you as having octopus arms, then we've got some work to do. I don't expect anyone to necessarily live in the perfect financial world I just described, but I do expect people to measure themselves against it for very important reasons. None of these reasons, by the way, includes materialism.

Metrics are important. They help us understand why certain things are and aren't. Why *haven't* we saved enough for retirement compared to how much we should have? Why *have* we accumulated more debt than the national average? Throughout our time together, I'm going to toss numbers and markers at you. Your goal shouldn't simply be to determine whether you've achieved the number or marker; instead, your aim should be to understand why, and more importantly *how*, that can change.

For instance, if you determine that you don't have enough money set aside for emergencies, you could either dismiss your newfound information with a tepid degree of apathy or ask yourself why that is and how you can change it. I'll provide as much of the *how you can change that* as possible; you just need to provide the *why*.

I've decided to do something quite odd in this particular book. I've decided to color the bookend chapters with the grave reality of what financial apathy looks like deep in your forties. In between, I've provided a step-by-step plan to make sure that your reality isn't the reality that I'll detail in both this chapter and Chapter 9, "The Plan."

If you're entering this book behind the proverbial eight ball, ideally you will leave with a practical strategy to change that.

YOU'RE IN A SANDWICH

You might be sandwiched by two sets of adults, neither of which is you. You've got your parents as the top bun and your (potentially) young adult children as the bottom bun. You're the meat. Sometimes being the meat isn't very much fun. And this is one of those instances.

While your main focus should be your financial life, you must be prepared to assist your parents in their financial planning, if for no other reason than to prevent their lack of planning from affecting you. And you must also make sure that once your children aren't children anymore, they launch successfully. You know, the old "I love you, but get out." I write that half-jokingly.

If you have children, you've undoubtedly learned how much financial complexity they can add to your life. If they're on the younger end of the scale, you may be faced with activity costs and college pre-funding. If they're on the other end of the scale, college funding and cutting the cord are in play.

Financially grounded children don't happen to you; you create them. They learn about money by watching you deal with money. Hey, the fact that you have a book called *Your Money Life: Your 40s* on the kitchen table may even show them how important it is to have a healthy relationship with money. If you experience financial trouble with your young adult children as they get older, their financial struggles are partially a product of your tutelage. Not exactly a fun pill to swallow.

Additional complexity arrives when you realize that your involvement in your parents' financial lives may at some point need to be necessary again. But this time they're not helping you—it may be time for you to focus on them.

Whether or not it's happened already, you will eventually switch roles with your parents. They will look to you for guidance. They will look to you for care. And they may even look to you to help them financially. This is inevitable in one way, shape, or form. I'd be lying if I told you that it isn't sad. It *is* sad. We're only talking about it because it can have a serious impact on your financial life.

No one really knows how to retire. Most people have never done it before. So when the time comes to retire—or in other words, when it comes time to give up your earned income—many mistakes can be made. People often retire too early, with too many expenses, and without a healthcare plan in place. But what do you care? You're in your forties, so you have your own things going on. You are getting married, having kids, building careers, and so on. All you generally know about your parents' financial situation is that it's probably better than yours. And *this* is where the trouble begins.

We are relative thinkers. We hold ourselves in a certain regard, and we hold in high regard anyone who seems to be in a better spot than us. It's kind of odd, but that's what we do. If someone is relatively more successful than us, we generally remove the "relatively" and simply call them financially successful. This most often occurs with our parents. They generally have more stable jobs, they have bigger 401(k)s, and they don't have the same material expenses as the typical young American family. All this adds up to assuming that our parents will be fine when it comes to retirement. That's a mistake.

At first, it seems like none of your darn business. But it is. Well, it will be. You will most likely be dealing with your parents' estate when they pass away. You will liquidate their assets, pay their debts, and keep the rest. No matter how much money they have, this process is uncomfortable at best and awful at worst. If your parents are adequately prepared, it's hard. And if your parents *aren't* adequately prepared, then it's really, really hard. The sooner you have a conversation with your parents about their retirement and estate plans, the less the situation will impact your financial life. Remember, it's still going to be hard.

So how exactly are you to say, "Hey Pops, I want to make sure everything's cool when you die"? It's not as cut and dried as death. You actually want to make sure everything is cool if your parents live. That's the whole point. They need planning. They need retirement planning, long-term care planning, and estate planning. These are things that you and I generally don't think about on a daily basis. The best way to bring it up is with a casual, "Hey, can you walk me through your retirement plans so that I know what my job is?" That will inevitably raise a "Huh?" That "Huh?" is a good thing. It gives you a chance to say something like this: "I've been doing a lot of reading on financial stuff recently. I read something the other day about your parents' retirement and estate plans. It said that I should know what's going on so that I can step up when necessary."

See, that wasn't too awkward. Make sure your parents know how important it is to you to help them. You aren't doing their planning, you are simply trying to find out what their plans are. And if they don't have any plans, then badger them until they get it done. It's at this point in time when you realize you have officially switched roles with your parents. "Get your homework done. Clean your room. Take out the trash. Get your retirement, long-term care, and estate planning done so that you don't leave the entire family hanging."

Once you take care of one of the generations surrounding you, you'll have an open-face sandwich. Take care of the other one, and you'll just be meat, standing all alone with your financial past behind you and your financial future ahead of you. What to do now?

If you have the immense pleasure to focus on your financial life and your financial life alone, then you will need to do a comprehensive examination of each area of your financial life. That's what the meat of this book is. Now I'll tell you everything you need to know about financial life in your forties.

WHAT YOU WILL LEARN

From investing to getting out of debt permanently, there's a lot you need to know by the time you hit 50. The next seven chapters will fill your financial cup with knowledge and action plans. Here are the specifics of what you will learn.

DEBT

Your attitude toward debt is direct product of your upbringing. You need to understand how to properly leverage debt and how to avoid thinking you *are* properly leveraging debt when in reality you aren't. Debt isn't evil, but a casual attitude toward debt can render your financial life miserable.

You will learn exactly what debt is good, what debt is bad, and most importantly, exactly the best way to pay off debt. You will learn why momentum matters more than math and why spraying all of your debts with "extra" money isn't very efficient. But most importantly, you will learn that if you handle your housing expenses properly, you will have zero debt by the time you get to retirement, and that includes mortgage debt.

SPENDING

The demands for your money will only increase more over time. As your family dynamic changes, so will your spending habits. Learning to avoid ruts, fight off apathy, and consistently care about your financial behavior is both challenging and vital. Unequivocally, your forties will be the most financially challenging decade of your life. You can lessen the impact of the demands of your forties by making spending rules for yourself in your thirties.

Control your spending, and you will be able to control your financial life. If you don't have control over your spending, you'll never make enough money to fund your lifestyle. One of the end goals of financial wellness is resourcefulness.

As you will learn, it's okay to occasionally splurge and buy something you normally wouldn't buy. In fact, learning when to splurge and when not to splurge will help you keep your financial stress in check. You've heard a thousand times why you should watch how much you dine out and spend on utilities, but this time I'll show you exactly how to do it while still living a normal life. We'll discuss when moderation is best and when it's best thrown out the window.

BUDGETING

You can't earn your way out of the need to budget. You can't make so much money that decision-making becomes unimportant. You'll learn how over-housing can create serious problems that affect your life for decades, and you'll learn how reducing your obligations will make retirement much easier than you thought it could be.

You will learn exactly how much of your take-home pay should go toward each budget category, including housing, transportation, food, and entertainment. You will learn why awareness, communication, and accountability are the keys to budgeting.

MAJOR PURCHASES

The success of your financial life will be determined based on your ability to make wise spending decisions on purchases both big and small. Budgeting will help you address the small decisions, but you'll need a comprehensive major-purchase strategy to stay out of big trouble. Your car and home purchases are tricky, given lenders' willingness to put you in an objectively rough financial situation.

You will learn exactly how much house and car you can afford, and better yet, when and how to finance the purchases.

CREDIT

One of the trickiest things you will learn in this book is the role that credit plays in our lives. While you certainly want to have good credit, you don't want to fall prey to the credit-score manipulation advice that floods the financial marketplace. As you will learn, your focus should be on developing and maintaining healthy credit habits, not just on trying to get your score to go up.

Your goal isn't to be good at borrowing money; it is to not *need* to borrow money. Credit scores trick us into becoming good borrowers. Healthy credit and financial habits allow us to not borrow.

SAVING AND INVESTING

You aren't likely to have a pension, and the Social Security retirement system has to change to stay solvent. Your financial independence (retirement) depends on your ability to save and invest your income.

You will learn how to save and invest, and you will learn why you need to get started yesterday. Additionally, you will learn that saving and investing aren't necessarily about accumulation as much as they're about breaking dependency on income. Retirement gets easier when you don't have substantial income needs.

INSURANCE

Insurance is a necessary evil. Various types of insurance, such as renters, auto, life, and disability, allow us to live our lives without worrying about events we can't control. Insurance will have your back, especially if you educate yourself on what types you need.

Your insurance needs will change throughout your life. You will learn what coverages you need in your forties and what coverages you can worry about later.

A PLAN

Life will throw you all sorts of financial curveballs. But if you have a plan, you will be prepared for not only the good times, but also the bad times. You will have a step-by-step action plan for what to do next. If you are motivated to better your financial life, I've got good news for you: Your motivation plus an action plan will equal financial progress. And that's why you got this book, right?

YOUR REMOVABLE GUIDE

Although it would be great if you could walk around with this book all the time, it's not exactly practical or realistic. What *is* realistic, though, is giving you a functional, focused, and powerful guide to keep track of your goals, progress, and information. Enter the *Your Money Life* guide.

A budget is worthless if you never look at it. Your financial goals are pointless if you never measure your progress toward them. And the power of your net worth goes untapped if you don't track it. The *Your Money Life* guide allows you to do all of these things in one convenient location.

GET STARTED

Your ability to juggle money to tend to your past, present, and future will determine your financial success. We're constantly told to live in the now and to plan for the future. But to do that, we must address our past. So regardless of whether it stresses you out, it's time to open the door to your past financial decisions and explore your debts.

CHAPTER 2

THE PAST: DEBT

Debt stinks for many reasons, but among the top reasons, you will find that debt forces you to live in the past when you would much rather live in the present and prepare for your future.

But it's not enough to rectify your current debts. You must also decide whether you want to be part of the debt game in the future. You don't *have to* borrow money. Sure, you are likely to borrow money if you choose to buy a house, but other than that, do you really need to borrow money? Because once you decide that borrowing is for you, you become part of a nasty little statistic.

The average American household had roughly $7,000 in consumer debt in 2013. But when you remove the households that have zero consumer debt, something interesting happens. The average household with *any* consumer debt has more than $15,000 in consumer debt. Basically, once you decide to make consumer debt a part of your life, you are likely to jump deep into the waters of debt. It's like smoking—once you decide you're going to be a smoker, you open your life up to the health statistics that come with being a smoker.

Debt levels in the United States have grown at a ridiculous pace as more and more consumers have decided that they want to play the debt game. In 1943, there was more than $6.5 billion in outstanding consumer credit. As of June 2014, there is $3.2 trillion of outstanding consumer credit.[1] And while I'm sure some of the $3.2 trillion worth of consumer debt is at 0

---

[1] http://www.federalreserve.gov/releases/g19/hist/ cc_hist_sa_levels.html.

percent interest, the vast majority of that debt costs borrowers a significant amount of money. You can't forget that when you borrow, the interest rate you pay makes the item(s) you are purchasing more expensive. A $20,000 car will cost you $21,675.89 when you finance it for 48 months with a 4 percent interest rate. That's 8.4 percent more than you have to pay.

What about a house? A $200,000 house will cost you $343,739.01 when you finance it for 30 years with a 4 percent interest rate. Choosing to utilize debt in this scenario causes you to pay 72 percent more for the house than you would have to if you had the money to pay cash.

Borrowing money doesn't just allow you to make a purchase you want to make; it changes the economics of the purchase itself.

THE CHEAP-MONEY FALLACY

People sell themselves all sorts of fuzzy logic when it comes to debt. Among the fuzziest you will find is the cheap-money fallacy. It's not uncommon to hear someone say, "I financed the car because the money was so cheap." What this person is trying to communicate is that he or she happens to believe the interest rate associated with the loan is relatively low. But low compared to what?

I recently met a 28-year-old who had done a tremendous job saving money. He had more than $35,000 saved in his checking and savings accounts. He also had a car payment. I was dismayed when he told me he didn't pay cash for his car because he was able to borrow the money for the car at 1.9 percent interest, therefore it was "cheap money." I understand his point. Borrowing money at 1.9 percent compared to 6 percent does in fact make it "cheaper," but the whole theory behind cheap money is more about the cash. It's only really cheap money if you do something better with the money you're not using to pay cash for the car. His $35,000 was earning less than 0.02 percent interest.

It doesn't make sense to pay any interest, however small the amount, if the cash you could have used to buy the car isn't gaining its own interest. The interest rate of the loan has to be relative to the rate of return you are receiving on other funds. Of course, you shouldn't go out and borrow money to invest it; that's a dangerous game. My issue is more that this guy's cash was just sitting in a checking account earning nothing. If he had told me the money he could have used for the car was earning an average of 6 percent each year, then fine—good for him. But it wasn't, so his "cheap money" idea didn't quite play out. Instead, he's paying 4 percent more for the car than he needed to.

Many debt problems arise when a consumer tries to get cute and play with logic. You can't out-math math. Paying 4 percent more for a purchase when you have the means to pay for the purchase outright doesn't make any sense at all.

TYPES OF DEBT

There are several different types of debt, and many of them have unique characteristics. It's imperative that you know how each type of debt works, the truths surrounding the debts, and where the type of debt falls on the Good Debt/Bad Debt scale.

The Good Debt/Bad Debt scale is an admittedly subjective scale on which you can begin to measure the utility of each different type of debt. A 1 on the Good Debt/Bad Debt scale indicates that there is close to zero sense in having or holding that type of debt. A 5 on the scale indicates that you're properly leveraging debt to improve your overall financial standing. I'm not going to go so far as to say there are good debts. But I will admit some debts are relatively better to hold than others.

For instance, I think a mortgage is the best debt to have, on a relative basis. But I'd rather you not have a mortgage at all. I don't really care about deducting the mortgage interest on your taxes. If you didn't have a mortgage payment, then your cash flow would still net positive compared to having a mortgage payment and deducting the mortgage interest on your taxes.

Consider this: If your gross household income is $80,000 and you pay $5,000 in mortgage interest, then your taxable income will become $75,000, after you've claimed the mortgage interest deduction on your tax return. Now, let's say you have a marginal tax rate of 25 percent. Your mortgage interest deduction just saved you $1,250 in taxes. I've got to admit, that's pretty awesome. You paid $5,000 in interest and reduced your taxes by $1,250, for a net outflow of $3,750. Let's now consider the alternative.

If you don't have any mortgage interest to deduct, your taxable income will remain $80,000. You don't get to legally avoid $1,250 in taxes, but you also don't have to pay $5,000 in mortgage interest. Whereas having mortgage interest to deduct (in our previous example) results in a net cash outflow of $3,750, having no mortgage interest to deduct results in a net cash outflow of $0. The choice is simple. If you keep a mortgage so that you can deduct the interest, you will pay a net amount of $3,750. If you don't have a mortgage, you will pay nothing.

The "keeping a mortgage to deduct the interest expense" myth is another example of trying to out-math math.

We will discuss the proper way to pay off your debts later in this chapter, but you should feel especially compelled to pay off your debts that fall on the low end of the Good Debt/Bad Debt scale. That being said, don't be dismissive of the debts you have on the top end of the Good Debt/Bad Debt scale.

STUDENT LOANS

It's quite possible that you still have some student loan debt hanging around. At this point in your life, you can't afford to be financially tied to your education, especially if it took place 20 years ago. You need to use the money you are paying toward your student loans for your other financial priorities, including retirement.

While student loans certainly don't have some of the nasty interest rates that can come with credit card debt, the monthly obligation is something you need to eliminate.

Good Debt/Bad Debt rating: 2 (because you are in your forties)

Analysis: One of the main considerations in your decision to take on student-loan debt was the possibility of an increased income due to a higher level of education and functional aptitude. If you played your cards right (and took out the right amount of debt for the quality and relevance of education purchased), then you made an investment in your future. In essence, you leveraged debt properly. And while your decision to borrow money was potentially both wise and admirable, you should still be diligent in your efforts to pay it back. The added complications of being in your forties arrive when you consider that you may soon be on the hook for someone else's college costs.

Federal (subsidized) student loans

- ▶ You didn't need a credit check to obtain federal student loans. Yet these loans can help you establish healthy credit.

- ▶ The nature of a subsidized loan is that the government will pay the interest payments on the loan for students with financial needs while the borrower is still at least a half-time student.

- ▶ You don't have a cosigner on your federal loans.

- ▶ You don't have to start repaying your federal loans until you are no longer classified as a student (you graduate, leave school, or switch to being less than a half-time student).

- ▶ Interest rates are fixed and are generally lower than the rates on private student loans.

Private student loans

▶ No one pays the interest on private student loans but you. There are no interest subsidies.

▶ Interest rates are variable and can approach 20 percent.

▶ Many private student loans require you to start making payments while you are still in school.

▶ You have to qualify for private loans via your credit score or a cosigner.

While many student-loan programs will allow you 25 years to repay your debts, you shouldn't take this long. Ten years is the standard loan-repayment period for a reason. Get your education and then pay it off. Don't live with student-loan debt for a quarter century just because you are allowed to.

PARENT STUDENT LOANS

Feel free to skip this section if you won't be in the position to have a college-age student. Better yet, don't skip it. You are going to learn about one of the biggest problems affecting retirement planning today.

Seventy-one percent of college seniors who graduated in 2013 had student loans. The average balance of the student loans was roughly $30,000. Student loans are available either through the federal government or through your university/college, bank, or credit union, usually as part of a financial-aid package.

Student loans are among the most substantial types of debt for recent college graduates, and they are becoming more common for parents, too. According to a study cited in *The Wall Street Journal*, over the last decade the average student loan debt in the United States has increased significantly—from roughly $18,000 in 2004 to $33,000 in 2014. The percentage of students graduating with debt has also risen from 64 percent in 2004 to 71 percent in 2014.[2]

Parent student loans—or Parent PLUS Loans, as they're often called—are loans that parents take out for their children's college education. When students begin the matriculation process—and yes, I just wanted to use the word *matriculation*—families often turn to the Free Application For Student Aid (FAFSA) form to seek financial aid. The FAFSA helps determine what a family's Expected Family Contribution (EFC) is. The EFC determines how much financial aid a family receives. I know—lots of acronyms and lots of confusion. But simply put, it works like this: A college provides a family a Cost Of Attendance (COA) number, the FAFSA determines the family's EFC, and then the COA minus the EFC determines a family's eligibility for need-based aid. Okay, fine, it's not simple.

Need-based aid includes programs such as Pell Grants, Perkins Loans, and direct student loans (borrowed by students). What if a family doesn't get enough need-based aid? That's where programs such as Parent PLUS Loans come into play. If a family has a solid household income, reasonable assets, and not a tremendous number of college-age children, they won't get the amount of need-based aid they might desire.

---

[2] http://blogs.wsj.com/numbers/congatulations-to-class-of-2014-the-most-indebted-ever-1368.

Good Debt/Bad Debt rating: 2

Analysis: It is not my intent to be controversial in giving parent student loans a 2 on the Good Debt/Bad Debt rating scale. My intent is to help you understand the impact Parent PLUS Loans can have on *your* financial life. Whether or not you choose to pay for your children's education clearly is your decision to make. Just know that there are many better ways to accomplish your goal than borrowing to pay for your kids' education. We'll discuss those strategies later in the book.

Default rates on Parent PLUS Loans have skyrocketed.[3] In 2006, 1.8 percent of Parent PLUS borrowers were in default. By 2010, default rates nearly tripled to 5.1 percent. Tripled! And this on the heels of tougher requirements. The increased scrutiny on parents' credit scores has saved many parents from being potential default cases as well.

BANK CREDIT CARD DEBT

Consumer credit tools can be traced back to the 1800s, when oil companies and general merchants extended credit to their individual consumers. It wasn't until the 1960s that a national system for accepting credit cards was implemented. The companies we now know as MasterCard and Visa were among the trailblazers of the consumer credit industry.

Credit cards are more prevalent today than ever before. This increased usage has led to a treasure trove of problems. High

---

[3] https://www.insidehighered.com/news/2014/04/03/education-department-releases-default-data-controversial-parent-plus-loans.

interest rates, penalties, and fees associated with your credit cards can quickly add up. Based on analysis of data provided by the Federal Reserve, the average American household owes $15,480 in credit card debt. The average college graduate owes close to $3,000.[4]

While many people might tell you that it's important to increase your credit score while you're in college and right after by using your credit cards early and often, it's much more important to focus on your financial health, not some arbitrary score that can take you down a nasty path. In fact, your credit score, that mystical metric that is often pointed to as the bastion of financial wellness, isn't a very good indicator of your financial health. Net worth, which is your assets minus your liabilities, paints a much clearer picture. Wouldn't you rather reduce your debts and increase your savings than manipulate an overrated number that just proves you are good at borrowing?

The good news is that a 2013 study by Fidelity suggested that credit card debt among recent college graduates is in decline. The 2009 Credit Card Reform Act is to blame for this. Or maybe I should say it is to be credited for this. College students can no longer be offered freebies on campus for opening up a credit card.

You'll notice that our discussion on credit cards will continue throughout this book. This is purposeful, the opposite of subtle, and the biggest hint you have ever been given.

---

[4] http://www.nerdwallet.com/blog/credit-card-data/ average-credit-card-debt-household.

Good Debt/Bad Debt rating: 1

Analysis: Why? Why do it? You don't need to. Save money, and then use the money to buy stuff you want. Don't borrow and then find a way to pay for it later. When you do that, you will end up paying more for your purchases. And for you "pay off your credit card at the end of each month" people, I've got a little something for you later in the book.

STORE CREDIT CARD DEBT

Nearly every major retailer—from Gap to Amazon to Walmart—offers customers the opportunity to apply for a credit card that can be used only in their store. They lure customers into signing up for their cards with an interest-free grace period (usually the first six months) or a discount on their purchases.

Consumers get into trouble when they neglect to pay off their balances—or when they use their cards beyond the interest-free grace period. Store credit cards offer high interest rates, many of them right around 25 percent. It doesn't take long for an interest rate that high to wreak havoc on someone's financial health. In addition, they do little to impact your credit score, and they have low limits, putting you at risk for added fees.

Store credit cards exist for one simple reason: to sell you more stuff. Every deal, coupon, or special offer is designed to induce spending, not help you. Store credit programs are created under the guise of loyalty programs, but who is being loyal to whom? In nearly every extreme debt situation I have ever encountered, store credit cards are present. They are a financial gateway drug.

Your best bet is to avoid store credit cards altogether. Signing up for a card to defer payment for an item over six months is a good indication that you shouldn't be buying that item in the first place.

Good Debt/Bad Debt rating: 1

Analysis: Store credit cards are as unnecessary as they are dangerous. They aren't collector cards. If your wallet has space for six credit cards, buy a smaller wallet. Don't fill up the wallet with store credit cards. Oh, and don't buy the wallet using a credit card.

CAR LOAN

Unless you live in the heart of a major city and have access to safe and affordable mass transit, chances are you're going to have to buy a car. While a car is arguably a necessity in the twenty-first century, it doesn't mean you have to disregard sensibility and contribute to the growing trend of skyrocketing car loans.

According to Experian Automotive, which tracks millions of auto loans written each quarter, the average amount borrowed by new car buyers in the fourth quarter of 2013 was a record-high $27,430. The average monthly payment for a new car was $471, and the average monthly payment for a used-car loan was $352.[5]

To make matters even worse, a record 20 percent of new-car loans were extended beyond six years. A car is one of the worst

---

[5] http://www.cnbc.com/id/101461972#.

investments you can make. It depreciates in value immediately after you drive it off the lot and continues to depreciate for the duration of the time you own it. Borrowing money to buy a depreciating asset isn't a great idea. By the mere fact that there is an interest charge associated with the loan, you are paying more for a car than it's worth, and when you have paid it off, it's worth even less.

Good Debt/Bad Debt rating: 3

Analysis: It's not the end of the world if you have car debt, but it's also not the best idea. If you ever find yourself underwater on a car (meaning you owe more on the car than it's worth), don't trade in the car and finance the entire process. You will drive off the lot owing more on your new car than it's worth, and your new car will instantly depreciate even further when you take it off the lot. Again, just because a car dealer will let you borrow $40,000 on a $30,000 car doesn't mean you should do it.

HOME LOAN (MORTGAGE)

At some point in the near future, you'll more than likely consider buying your first home. Home ownership is, after all, part of the American Dream. Home ownership is also the number-one reason why many Americans carry the burden of debt for the majority of their lives.

As you will learn in Chapter 5, "The Possessions: Major Purchases," the type of mortgage you get is incredibly important. A mortgage can be a decent use of debt because the underlying asset (the house) is, generally speaking, an appreciating asset. An appreciating asset is an asset that goes up in value over time. So by the time you have paid off your mortgage, the home itself generally, but not always, will have increased in value.

Good Debt/Bad Debt rating: 5

Analysis: A home is an asset that is easily exchanged in a reasonable marketplace. You don't necessarily have to wait until the end of your mortgage term to profit on the buying and selling of a house. Of any debt you could ever possibly acquire, this is the best one. But remember, we're comparing a mortgage to the likes of credit cards and payday loans.

MEDICAL DEBT

Rising medical costs and insurance premiums have made medical debt the number-one cause of bankruptcy filings in the United States, according to a recent study from NerdWallet Health. More than 1.7 million Americans will file bankruptcy because of unpaid medical bills in the next year, and 56 million adults—more than 20 percent of the population between 19 and 64—will struggle with medical debt. In an attempt to pay off their debt, more than 11 million people will increase their credit card debt as well.

While preparing for medical debt can be difficult—especially as a young person at the peak of his or her physical health—building up a significant emergency savings fund and funding a Health Savings Account (HSA), when applicable, can help offset the financial repercussions of medical expenses.

Anecdotally, medical debt has always seemed to me to be the most ignored. I've witnessed a great number of people exhibit outright dismissive attitudes about medical debt. You'll learn more about how to protect yourself from medical debt in Chapter 8, "The Pitfalls: Insurance."

Good Debt/Bad Debt rating: 4

Analysis: While you shouldn't carry medical debt, if you happen to acquire some due to medical issues, you shouldn't panic. Your health is very important, and if you make wise health-care decisions, you can feel justified in spending money on improving your health. Medical debt tends to bring quite a bit of stress, because of the residual stress associated with the root medical problem. Do not interpret a rating of 4 on the Good Debt/Bad Debt scale as justification to ignore your medical debts. However, if there is a debt about which you truly don't have a choice, it's medical debt. Take it seriously.

LINES OF CREDIT (SECURED AND UNSECURED)

A line of credit is different from a loan in that it's not one lump sum of money. Instead, you can draw from a specified amount of money in your line of credit in the same way that you would use a credit card. There are two types of lines of credit: secured and unsecured.

A secured line of credit is one that is backed by collateral, such as a house or another piece of property. An unsecured line of credit is one that has no collateral backing it up. Because unsecured lines of credit are riskier for lenders, their interest rates are significantly higher than secured lines of credit.

Both are risky for borrowers, and for different reasons. If you can't pay back your secured line of credit, you put yourself at risk of losing whatever collateral you've offered up. If you can't pay back your unsecured line of credit, high interest rates can add up quickly. Be very careful when tapping a line of credit, which can certainly have a blank-check quality to it.

It's not uncommon for homeowners to tap their equity line of credit to make home improvements. Sometimes the home improvements increase the underlying property value, and sometimes they don't. You've heard it a million times, and in case you haven't, let me say it again: Your house is not a piggy bank. Removing equity from your home, even to theoretically increase the value of your home via home-improvement projects, is a bad idea. Home-improvement projects very rarely equal a dollar-for-dollar increase in home value. That $15,000 landscaping job you just completed probably did close to nothing for the value of your home.

Good Debt/Bad Debt rating: 2

Analysis: If you own a home, you will be presented with the opportunity to rob your home of its equity. Sure, it's called a home equity line of credit (HELOC), and it sounds innocuous. But it's not. It doesn't make sense to borrow against an asset you've already established. Use your income to push your financial life forward. Don't tap the assets you've already worked so hard to build. When you take out a line of credit, you will run in place financially.

401(k) LOANS

Your employer may allow you to borrow against your retirement plan. Don't do it. There are several handfuls of reasons why you shouldn't borrow against your future. I'll highlight some of the biggest ones.

Most 401(k) loans must be paid back in less than five years. The interest rate is relatively low, and the participant does end up paying the interest to himself. But the "paying yourself" interest argument is the equivalent of driving 90 miles to get cheap gas.

You should also know that if you leave your current job, your 401(k) loan will become payable immediately. This means that if you can't pay, you will owe taxes because your loan will be classified as a nonqualified withdrawal. And don't forget the 10 percent penalty you will owe if you are younger than 59-1/2.

Let's say you want to borrow money to pay off some out-of-control credit card debt that has accumulated. Credit card debt is a manifestation of your past. When you rectify your past (debt) with your future (401(k)), magic isn't the result. Two wrongs don't make a right. It's actually two bad decisions stacked on top of each other. If you took a $10,000 loan on January 1, 2013, to pay off your credit card debt, then you would have shielded $10,000 from a 30 percent growth year (the S&P 500 return). Sure, you paid yourself some paltry amount of interest, but you missed out on a 30 percent return.

Often, borrowers are also disallowed from making new contributions to a retirement plan while they have an outstanding loan balance. Don't forget, time is your other precious financial resource. The longer you go without making contributions to your retirement plan, the more challenging your retirement plan becomes.

Good Debt/Bad Debt rating: 2

Analysis: You cannot sell out your future for your present or past. There is no more tangible example of this sell-out process than a 401(k) loan. Parents often turn to retirement plans to help fund their children's college educations; they shouldn't. Two of the largest financial events in a person's life are retirement and a college education. It's unadvisable to sacrifice a retirement, which cannot be financed, for an education, which can be financed. And by the way, if anyone should finance a college education, it should be the person who receives value from said education.

PERSONAL LOANS (FROM A FINANCIAL INSTITUTION)

A personal loan is an unsecured loan (meaning that you don't have to put up any collateral) granted for personal use. You might secure a personal loan to help pay for everything from medical expenses to replacing your home's air conditioner to covering college costs.

The loan amount is determined by your credit history and your income—essentially, your ability to pay back your lender. Because no collateral is involved, your interest rates will be much higher.

Good Debt/Bad Debt rating: 2

Analysis: It's possible you will need to take a personal loan from a bank, but you should try to avoid it. A personal loan is similar to a secured or an unsecured equity line, except a personal loan isn't open-ended and can have a shorter amortization schedule.

PERSONAL LOANS (FROM A FAMILY MEMBER OR FRIEND)

Do you love your family and friends? (The correct answer is yes.) Then why make your financial problems their financial problems? Personal loans from family and friends, whether formal or informal, are a bad idea. If a lending institution isn't willing to loan you money because of your credit-(un)worthiness, why subject your loved ones to your objectively high level of lending risk?

Your family and friends may offer to help you out financially, but unless it's life or death, say no. Relationships should not be splintered for avoidable financial reasons.

Given that you are somewhere between 20 and 30 years removed from living with your parents as a minor, it's time to cut the cord.

Good Debt/Bad Debt rating: 1

Analysis: Avoid both sides of the personal loans from friends or family equation. You will almost always come away disappointed.

TAX DEBT

Tax debt happens when you fail to pay earned income taxes to the state or federal government. In addition to the debt total, depending on the severity of the situation, you could incur fines and penalties (including jail time) for delayed payments.

If tax debt goes unpaid for long enough, the IRS has the right to garnish your wages until the debt is paid off. You might also have the ability to set up a payment plan with the IRS to pay off your debt in installments.

The moral of the story? Make sure you know how to calculate your personal and business taxes—or hire someone who can. That investment will more than offset the costs incurred from tax debt. You want stress? Owe the IRS back taxes. You want to avoid financial stress? Start by keeping current with your taxes. You don't want to go down the tax-debt road. It's a dead end.

Good Debt/Bad Debt rating: 1

Analysis: Did you read the part of this section that said jail time? Jail time is an automatic 1 on the Good Debt/Bad Debt rating scale.

COLLECTION DEBT

If you are unable to pay a bill, the lender can send it directly to a debt-collection agency. As a result, you'll begin to receive phone calls and letters from collectors in the weeks following your first missed payment. If you owe a substantial amount of money, debt collectors can take extreme measures—such as filing judgments—to ensure that you repay the debt.

Being unable to pay a bill is stressful in the first place; being sent to collections adds another level of financial stress that can affect your entire life.

Good Debt/Bad Debt rating: 1

Analysis: A strange yet common reaction to having debt go to collections is to ignore the collection calls. Don't ignore the collection calls. Unfortunately, when a debt goes to collections, you will lose leverage. The collection agents are generally compensated based on the amount of money they can collect from you. To move on with your financial life, you must right things with the collection companies that hold your debts. Don't let it get this far—but if it does, deal with it quickly.

JUDGMENTS

Judgments are legal obligations to pay a debt or damages that have been issued in a court of law. If a creditor takes you to court and is awarded a judgment, it gives the creditor the right to use additional methods to collect the debt they are owed, including wage garnishment, liens, and levies.

Wage garnishment involves an automatic deduction from your paycheck—up to 25 percent—each pay period. This money is sent directly to your judgment creditor until the debt is paid off.

The judgment process is quite nasty. Creditors often provide delinquent borrowers with a summons to appear in court. The hope for the creditors is that the borrower doesn't show up to court. When a borrower misses his or her time in front of a judge, the creditor is given a default judgment. This is when wages can be garnished. Creditors have been known to consistently seek continuances when borrowers actually show up for court, in order to increase the chances that a borrower won't show up for the next hearing. The second a borrower doesn't show up in court, a default judgment is made. A creditor's goal is to get a default judgment. Your goal is to not get anywhere close to being in this situation. And if you are in this situation, show up for court. Don't let a default judgment occur.

When a lien is placed on your home or your property, you will have to pay the debt with the money you earn from selling or refinancing the assets that have liens.

If the judgment creditor is awarded a levy, they can take funds directly from your checking or savings account—or even levy your personal property and sell it in an auction—to pay off the debt.

Good Debt/Bad Debt rating: 2

Analysis: Look, judgments aren't great. And I understand that having your wages garnished is both frustrating and embarrassing, but at least you'll get out of debt. Don't get me wrong; you should avoid letting your debts get so out of control that a judge is involved, but there is a silver lining to having your debts go to judgment: You will finally deal with the obligation you've been fighting or ignoring. You can't make progress when you're in denial. A judgment flips the denial switch to reality.

A CLOSER LOOK AT DEBT AND PAYING IT DOWN

Every bad habit comes equipped with a healthy dose of denial. Debt is no different. Over the years, I've compiled a mental archive of the different ways people try to rationalize their debt or blame it on someone else. Here are some of the most common:

▶ My finances were in good shape until I got those unexpected medical bills in the mail.

▶ I had to take out student loans because I didn't have a job.

▶ The TV was on sale. I would have been silly not to buy it at that price.

▶ My car was out of warranty, and I hate driving a car that isn't under warranty.

▶ I was throwing money away by renting, so it only made sense to buy a house.

▶ I wanted to build credit, so I opened a store credit card. And then it got a bit out of control.

The list goes on. But no matter how good your excuse is, there's no gray area when it comes to debt—you're either in it or you're not. And if you're in it, it can only be tackled through discipline, patience, and proper planning. As you begin to think about your debt, remember one thing: A debt is a debt is a debt. Don't ignore the "12 months same as cash" debt you accrued when you bought your new couch on the promise of no interest for a year. Don't ignore your student loans, even if they're in deferment. (While deferment does allow you to delay your payments, doing so simply puts off the inevitable.) If you owe money to any company, person, or other entity, it counts toward your debt total. Compartmentalizing your debt into arbitrary categories merely detracts from your progress.

Although I'm dedicating only one chapter to the creation of your debt pay-down plan, it could take months or even years to get completely out of debt, depending on the amount of debt you have. Don't be discouraged by the impending hard work, though; this plan will get you on a regular payment schedule, make your financial stress progressively easier to manage, and prepare you for your retirement income.

YOUR RELATIONSHIP WITH DEBT

Let's not be obtuse and suggest that all debt is bad. Debt exists in a person's life for several reasons. It may exist due to a lack of preparedness. It may exist due to poor behavior and decision-making. And it may exist as a reasonable strategy. But no matter the reason, debt consistently does one not-so-good thing: It obligates you to your past. In fact, every time you make the decision to go into debt, your current self is creating a relationship with your future self. It's hard enough to fund both your current lifestyle and your future life. If you throw in a relationship with your past financial decisions, then watch out.

DEBT PAY-DOWN PROCESS

People use three primary strategies to pay off debt. One of these strategies is effective; the other two strategies are commonly used yet often fall short. You must understand all three strategies, which we'll discuss in a moment, to understand why one strategy is the best.

Paying down debt is challenging for several reasons, but the two hardest parts are your battle against human nature and your simultaneous attack on your financial past, present, and future.

Before you get started with your debt pay-down, you need to understand a very important piece of the debt-reduction puzzle: You must stop using debt as a tool. It's impossible to get out of debt if you keep trickling back into debt each month by using your credit card. Stop using your bank credit card, store credit card, and/or line of credit. You won't be able to stay afloat if there's a hole in your boat.

Your commitment not to use debt as a tool will require sacrifice. Your credit card may have allowed you to buy some time in the past, but the time you bought came at a serious price. Now it's time to pay the piper.

Once you've committed to not using your credit cards, you are ready to get out of debt. The three most popular methods of paying off debt are the *math* method, the *momentum* method, and the *shotgun* method. Do you know which one is best?

THE MATH METHOD

Because debt deals with numbers, you'd think math would and should be involved in paying off debt. Well, it is, but at some point it makes sense to ignore the math and focus on your behavior instead. We'll talk more about that in a bit.

To be fair, the math method is technically the best way to pay off debt. But I find it to much less effective than other methods. The reality is, if you were so good at operating in purely mathematical terms, would you have all that debt in the first place? Probably not.

When using the math method of paying off debt, you focus on attacking the debt that has the highest interest rate. Each debt that you have has its own interest rate. Some of your debts may have interest rates less than 10 percent, some in excess of 10 percent, and some interest rates even skyrocket past 30 percent. The higher the interest rate, the more money you will end up paying your creditors if you continue to stay in debt to them. This higher borrowing cost over time causes many people to attack their debts with the highest interest rates first. And technically, they are doing the right thing. The faster they pay down the high-interest debts, the less interest they'll pay on those debts. It's textbook perfect. But human nature is a fickle beast.

Paying off your past financial decisions can prove so difficult and time consuming that you may abandon a successful strategy if you don't feel you're getting the results you desire in a timely manner. Behavior change needs to be reinforced. If you've shifted your financial habits to throw more money toward your debts, you want to see tangible, powerful results, right? Consider the following scenario.

You have two $2,000 debts. One is a car loan at 2.9 percent interest, and the other debt is a credit card at 29.99 percent interest. Which debt would you focus on paying off first? When I say "focus on," I mean paying more than the minimum required payment.

For this example, let's assume you have an additional $200 per month you could put toward one of your debts. If you used the highest interest rate method, you would attack the credit card, because its rate is 27.09 percent more than the car loan interest rate. But what do you think the minimum payment is for the credit card? Maybe $70 or so? Now, what do you think the payment on the car loan is? For the sake of the example, let's say $300. If you were to pay off the car loan first, you would free up $300 per month of cash flow. If you were to pay off the high-interest credit card first, you'd free up $70 per month of cash flow.

By ignoring the interest rates, you would be able to access $300 faster than you could access $70. Additionally, if you had been paying the $200 extra toward your car loan, then you would have been making $500 payments. You would already be used to living without the $500 with regard to discretionary spending, so you could simply start paying $570 per month toward your credit card balance once your car loan was paid off.

And just like that, you've dipped your toe into the waters of the momentum method….

THE MOMENTUM METHOD

The momentum method of paying off debt has been around for years, and people call it many different things. I call it the momentum method. It takes advantage of human behavior and engagement. Many people give up on their debt-repayment strategy because they don't see the fruits of their labor. The momentum method ensures that you will see your debts start to shrink in a dramatic and impactful way.

In a nutshell, the momentum method requires you to make minimum payments on all your debts, except your smallest-balance debt. You should then aggressively attack the smallest-balance debt, paying as much toward it as possible. Once it's eliminated, take its minimum payment and use it to focus on the next smallest debt, along with all the other income you've dedicated to debt repayment. Continue attacking the smallest-balance debt until all your debts are eliminated.

I prefer the momentum method and fully endorse it. I'll fully explain how it works after you understand the shotgun method.

THE SHOTGUN METHOD

Shotguns are effective because when you pull the trigger once, your target area is riddled with shot. The idea is that by peppering the target area, you are more likely to hit the intended specific target. A rifle, on the other hand, gives you one shot to hit the intended target. Yet from a distance, a rifle is a much more powerful weapon. Don't spray your debt from a distance with lots of little pellets.

The shotgun method of debt is when you attack many debts at once. Specifically, you pay more than the minimum payment on several different debts. I know you've always heard that you *should* pay more than your minimum payments on all your different debts, but you shouldn't. You will get out of debt much faster if you focus all of your extra payments toward your lowest-balance debt.

People who use the shotgun method often describe a sensation of running in place. A few years ago I met a nurse who was paying extra on all her different debts. She had nine credit cards, a car loan, and three medical bills. She was paying $1,500 per month toward her debts, yet she hadn't made much progress in more than two years. Upon discovering that she was using the shotgun method, we changed her strategy to the momentum method and ran some quick projections. In just two short months using the momentum method, she paid off five debts and freed up $450 of cash flow per month.

GETTING OUT OF DEBT

Eliminating a debt means eliminating a minimum payment. The faster you eliminate a debt, the faster you get to recapture its minimum payment. Because of this, your goal is to pay off debts as quickly as possible. The fastest way to do this is to attack the smallest-balance debt first. Here's how it works.

STEP 1: MAP OUT YOUR DEBT

Before you decide how you're going to pay off your debt, you need to figure out what debt you actually have. If you are in a bit of denial over your debts, you may have never compiled a comprehensive list. To do this, list all of your debts, from the smallest balance to the largest balance, in Table 2.1. Allow yourself as much time as necessary to complete this table—and make sure not to leave out any details. Remember to list every type of debt. This includes credit cards, mortgages, car loans, student loans, personal loans, and even debts that have made their way to collections.

STEP 2: BUILD MOMENTUM WITH SMALL DEBT VICTORIES

Don't make equal payments on each debt; it's inefficient. Employing this strategy may have been your problem for years. It's not unusual for people to pay extra on all their debts. As you know, your debts have a required minimum payment. Many people do what they believe to be a good idea and pay more than the minimum payment on all their debts. Frustration eventually sets in because they don't appear to be making any progress toward their goal of being debt free.

Instead, you should focus on paying off your smallest debt and getting the balance down to zero. This will free up the money you were putting toward the monthly minimum payment so you can put it toward the next debt—not to mention it also helps you create a sense of financial momentum. You may start

Table 2.1: Map Out Your Debt			
Whom Do You Owe?	Amount Owed	Minimum Payment	New Monthly Payment

Table 2.1: Map Out Your Debt

Whom Do You Owe?	Amount Owed	Minimum Payment	New Monthly Payment

out by paying only $100 per month extra above the minimum payment. But by the end of the debt pay-down process, you might actually be putting upwards of $1,000 per month toward the next lowest debt balance. This scenario is possible because you have eliminated debts and are able to use former minimum payments to help you pay off the next debt.

If you're wondering why we're focusing on the lowest balance instead of the highest interest rate, it's because we're trying to create momentum and zero balances. So at this point, try not to concern yourself with the interest rates (even though I know that goes against conventional wisdom).

Creating small victories and zero balances up front is the financial equivalent of losing that first five pounds on a diet. You just need some confirmation that what you're doing really works. As you pay off these balances, you'll begin to accumulate the money you were once putting toward minimum payments each month, allowing you to apply those savings to the next lowest balance on your list.

STEP 3: COMMIT TO A DEBT-PAYMENT SCHEDULE

This process is as simple as it gets, assuming you commit to making it part of your routine. The key is to keep chipping away at the debt. Sure, it will take time, but it will also work. Every time you free up money in your budget, apply it to your next lowest balance.

As a personal finance expert, I'm always tempted to create complicated processes for debt liquidation. But the reality is you need a very simple plan that's easy to stick to. Debt liquidation is way too important to complicate it with confusing financial algorithms and impossible goals.

YOUR PERSPECTIVE NEEDS TO SHIFT

There's no doubt your debt is a hindrance. But if you shift your perspective, then this hindrance immediately becomes a legitimate opportunity. This isn't some sort of strange exercise in semantics. If you pay down your debt between now and your retirement date, it may actually put you in a better position over those that are spending a vast majority of their pre-retirement income on consumer habits that have been formed for a decade or more. Whereas those people are forcing themselves to quit a learned habit, you are employing brilliant, healthy habits as you head into your retirement.

People often take on debt payments based on consumer confidence. When your world is great, when the economy is singing and the market is climbing, most people feel confident. Confidence is a great thing, but what generally happens next isn't. Consumer confidence is used as an economic measure for economists because purchasing usually follows it. When confident, a person tends to spend money, not save money. When people lack confidence, they save money. I know; it's a terribly backward way of thinking. Don't waste confidence on creating more obligations. Harness confidence to improve your life, not your lifestyle.

WHAT NOW?

The fewer obligations you have, the less pressure you will put on your income. Your goal is to permanently eliminate as many (debt) obligations as possible. There is a hidden benefit to paying off your debts systematically using the momentum method. You will learn to live without the money you use to pay on your debts' principal and interest each month. The first month you are debt free will determine what's next for you and your financial life.

If, upon becoming debt free, you reabsorb the money you've put toward debt reduction, you'll waste a giant opportunity. The most dangerous month in your financial recovery is always the month after you become debt free, because if you form new habits with your new discretionary income, then you are creating new forms of obligations. Instead, focus on making the best use of your freed-up capital. Strengthen your emergency fund. Increase your contributions to your retirement plan. Do anything to move yourself forward. Don't create new obligations.

CHAPTER 3

THE PRESENT: SPENDING

I know what you're thinking. "Sweet! I know lots about spending money." Not to burst your bubble, but that's exactly what we need to discuss. We need to make sure you aren't *too* good at spending money. Spending money without tracking it is a bad idea. And once you track it, you need to adjust your habits.

You'll never know for sure what's going on with your money unless you track it. Controlling your cash flow is the single most financially responsible thing you can do. When people say you need to learn to walk before you learn to run, they are describing this very concept. Understanding cash flow is a fundamental financial baby step, yet it's the one thing people gleefully ignore.

Often, the more money you make, the more you ignore cash-flow management. When you feel broke, you usually do something about it (in other words, you monitor your cash flow). But when you feel financially prosperous, you may not feel as concerned about where your money goes. This principle is what typically prevents people who have increased their income from increasing their wealth.

Cash flow describes the flow of money into your household (income) and the flow of money out of your household (expenses). A positive net cash flow means you have more money coming in than going out, and a negative net cash flow means you have more money going out than coming in. These net cash flows are also known, respectively, as a *surplus* and a *shortage*.

In addition, it's important that you don't keep too much money at your disposal. Whether intentionally or accidentally, many people experience manufactured financial tranquility as a result of keeping too much money in their checking accounts. While this may sound like a good problem to have, it is dangerous. A checking account has a very low yield, meaning your money gains only a minimal amount of interest when instead it could be working for you. But more importantly and less obviously, keeping too much money at your disposal can ruin an otherwise perfectly good financial situation.

Let me explain by using my favorite bathroom resource—toilet paper—as an example. As unpleasant as it is to think about, we've all been faced with the alarming prospect of being stranded without the appropriate amount of toilet paper. It may sound humorous now, but it's extremely unfunny in the moment. The point is, faced with the cardboard, you will survive in any way possible, and you'll learn two lessons because of it:

▶ Check supply levels before you use the bathroom!

▶ Be resourceful.

It's easy to be wasteful when you have a full roll and you forget what you went through when faced with an empty roll.

The same thing can happen when you have a relatively large roll, er, balance in your checking account. This feeling of financial abundance can occur with as little as $100 or $200 "extra" in your checking account. The amount of money that causes this strangely damaging phenomenon is different for everyone. It all depends on at what amount you start to be relatively complacent.

Think about your checking account. At what point do you stop checking the balance in your head (or online) before making a purchase? When you have a cushion of $100? $200? $500? When you become comfortable with your cushion, your economic stress eases, and you start making spending decisions that aren't always prudent or even practical. This is what I like to call *abundance spending,* and it can manifest itself in several ways.

A feeling of financial comfort can lead you to buy items normally out of your price range for one very simple reason: You know you presently have the money to cover them. The larger the cushion you give yourself, the larger the financial mistakes you can make. For example, think about all of the celebrities and once-well-off public figures who have gone bankrupt. When you hear these stories, you wonder how someone who once had so much could now have next to nothing. I'm not a betting man (but you probably already knew that), but I'd guess that in 99 percent of these cases, abundance mentality played a very large role.

But back to the concept of cash flow. You can increase yours in two ways:

- ▶ Spend less money by controlling your expenses.
- ▶ Make more money.

Despite popular belief, more money is not always the solution to your financial problems. When you give an undisciplined person more money, he or she is likely to end up in financial trouble again. The solution to what ails you is not more money—it's spending less. So if you want to improve your monthly cash flow, start by cutting your expenses. Otherwise, you are filling your money bucket with more money...despite the fact that there is a hole in your bucket.

HOW USING A CREDIT CARD COMPLICATES SPENDING

I frequently encounter people who want to argue the "charge everything and pay it off at the end of the month" method with me. This method has a person put every single monthly expense, even utility bills, on his or her credit card and then make one big payment to pay off the credit card balance each month. People do this for several reasons, including earning credit card points, increasing their credit scores, and creating convenience. And while using this particular method of spending accomplishes all three of those things, it's still a bad idea.

The credit card usage proponents will tell you about all the rewards they earn. They'll tell you how they've paid for Christmas gifts with the rewards points they receive, and they'll go into great detail about how committed they are to paying off their entire balance at the end of each month. But what they don't realize is that their logic has failed them. The discipline that's required to pay off a card at the end of every month opens them up to a lack of financial accountability throughout the month. Their commitment to pay off their debt at the end of each month—no matter how much it is—is exactly what gets them in trouble.

Here's why:

▶ **People rarely check their credit card balance mid-month.** On the other hand, people who do most of their spending with their checking account generally check their account balances at least twice (and generally more like 10 times) per month. While monitoring your checking account balance isn't exactly the perfect way to watch your spending, it's much better than never checking your balance—especially if you're trying to live lean and cut spending.

People who charge everything and then worry about it later (at the end of the month) don't really care how much they've spent mid-month because they aren't in danger of having insufficient funds. The "charge everything and pay it off at the end of the month" people never approach their credit card limit during the course of the month. This means that spending habits gone awry aren't addressed until the behavior has passed.

This isn't good. You should study your spending habits. How? By monitoring your spending. Have you ever had one of those weeks where stress, a sense of abundance, or the commerce fairy has caused you to spend money like it was going out of style? Join the club. Everyone has. But when you charge everything and pay it off at the end of the month, you tend to ignore this problem until the billing cycle is over. No one ever goes on a three-day spending bender and then checks their credit card balance mid–billing cycle.

▶ **When you're using a credit card, spending is much less consistent.** Scarcity is one of the best financial tools on the planet. I personally use it all the time to accomplish very important personal financial goals. However, when you exclusively use your credit card to buy things, you kick scarcity out of the equation. What's your credit card limit? Five thousand dollars? Ten thousand? Fifteen thousand? That's about typical for someone who uses the "charge everything and pay it off at the end of the month" method.

For the sake of conversation, let's say you put $4,000 per month on your credit card. Because you plan on paying off your credit card bill at the end of the month, you have at least $4,000 in your checking account, right? And what is even more likely is that you have much more than $4,000 in your checking account prior to paying your mortgage and credit card bill. How do I know this? Because about 40 percent of your spending is discretionary spending. You know, the type of spending that you put on your credit card.

My point? Between your swollen checking account and your $15,000 credit limit, you have "access" to $25,000 per month. This is a drain on anyone's self-control. You can afford *anything* you want. It is my experience both as an individual consumer and as someone who studies money that this access is a very, very bad thing.

Right now you might be thinking, "No way, Pete. I've never even considered that I have access to $25,000." Yes you have. Your brain has. Let's say you go to your grandma's house for Thanksgiving dinner, and she has a bowl of M&Ms out for everyone to enjoy. In the first scenario, she has one four-ounce bag of M&Ms in a small dish for your entire family to pick at throughout the day. How do most people address this situation?

They pick up just a few M&Ms with their fingertips. In the second scenario, Grandma went to Costco. She has an entire three-gallon punchbowl filled with M&Ms. How do most people deal with this scenario? They jam their fist so far into the bowl that it looks like they're trying to rehab a shoulder injury. The large punchbowl filled with M&Ms will result in more consumption *every single time*. Yet your hunger never changed. *Nothing* changed except your snap judgment on the resources that were made available to you.

Scarcity will help you accomplish financial goals much more than abundance will. By the way, don't try to impress me with your giant credit limit. I'd be much more impressed if you didn't have a credit card at all.

▶ **You think you're beating the system.** Much like the guy who has a "system" for winning consistently at roulette, "charge everything and pay it off at the end of the month" people tend to think they are smarter than the house. The house *always* wins. Do you really think these multibillion-dollar companies with their marketing and consumer behavior research departments are giving you free stuff? Oh, come on. They are counting on you overspending—or better yet, they're waiting for your commitment to pay off your balance every month to fade. When it fades, then the interest clock starts. And don't think the credit card companies don't make money off of you if you pay off your balance. They have other revenue streams attached to your purchases, such as swipe fees.

Need more convincing? Okay, you asked for it.

Failed logic #1: I get 1 percent cash back on purchases. How is that bad?

Many credit card companies now offer you cash back on your purchases. This means that you'll receive somewhere between 1 and 3 percent of what you charge on the card in the form of a bill credit or a check from the credit card company. This is much less exciting than it seems. How much money do you spend each month on your credit card? Twenty-five hundred dollars? Thirty-five hundred? Let's say you put $2,500 per month on your credit card. What is 1 percent of $2,500? Twenty-five dollars. Wow, that's amazing. You received 25 whole American dollars for risking so much more.

What are the chances that you overspend by more than 1 percent each month on your credit card? I would say that chances are about 100 percent. As we discussed just a few moments ago, access to copious amounts of money is a bad thing when it comes to controlling spending. People who employ the "charge everything and pay it off at the end of the month" method tend to overspend by at least 10 percent per month. This means that your 1 percent or even 3 percent cash back is pointless. You are actually behind by between 7 and 9 percent per month. You'd be better off not using a credit card and mailing 5 percent of your money to the Easter Bunny.

Failed logic #2: I make enough money and spend enough money to make the rewards worth it.

Once again, high income doesn't necessarily mean you are a financial genius. It just means that you make a lot of money. So you have immediately said to yourself, "I spend much more than $2,500 on my credit card. I spend closer to $10,000 per month on my card." The percentages didn't change. Your cash back "reward" would be $100 per month, and your likely amount of financial waste would be $1,000 per month. You can't spend your way out of trouble. You cannot out-math math.

IF NOT A CREDIT CARD, THEN WHAT?

There once was a time when people balanced their checkbooks. It was called the 1980s. Back then, there were fewer ways to make a financial transaction. Your options were cash, check, and charge. You received your canceled checks in the mail, so you knew when your party was paid. The reality is we'd actually be in a better place if we still balanced our checkbooks, but most people don't. Technology has created convenience, and this convenience has created a new type of ignorance.

Two convenient yet overused items emerged in the 1990s: the fanny pack and the debit card. While the fanny pack certainly is convenient, its insistence that you store things much in the way a marsupial would leaves me wanting more out of my containment solutions. And the debit card is the height of convenience. If you don't have cash, you can put a purchase on the plastic, and it's automatically withdrawn from your checking account. You don't need to carry around a checkbook, and more than one accountholder can use the cards at the same time, in multiple locations.

You would think the only prerequisite would be having money in your checking account to cover the purchases. Alas, this isn't the case, because that would make too much sense. Why would a bank offer you convenience if it doesn't improve its bottom line? It generally wouldn't. Banks make billions of dollars every year on debit card fees and overdraft fees. Therefore, they will often let you spend money you don't have, charge you overdraft fees, and then create a massive debt that must be satisfied the next time you deposit money into your account.

Fast-food restaurants accept debit cards, carwashes accept debit cards, and even the telephone company accepts debit cards. Thanks to the debit card, the critical thinking that used to guide our financial decision-making has decreased, while our number of financial transactions has increased.

Think about how easy it is to let your life be dictated by your debit card. The convenience of the card often overshadows the problems it can create.

Here's how a day can go terribly wrong, thanks to your debit card: You wake up in the morning and head to work. Stopping at Starbucks, you buy a coffee for $4 with your debit card. Once at the office, you purchase some Girl Scout cookies from a co-worker's daughter; the $9 cookies also go on your debit card. You go to your favorite deli for lunch and spend $8.56 on your debit card. On the way back to the office, you stop to buy a birthday card for your Aunt Helen: $3.56 on your debit card. You then make travel arrangements for your vacation, putting $1,235.86 on your debit card. On your way home from work, you pick up dry cleaning for $21.74 on your debit card. You then stop and get a pizza for dinner for $15.87—another debit.

In just 12 hours' time, you have made seven transactions and spent $1,298.59. You may have the receipts in your pocket, but will you have them at the end of the day? Did you reconcile your check register? Did you accidentally overdraft and get hit with seven different overdraft charges? If you average three transactions a day for a month, are you going to keep track of 93 transactions as they relate to your monthly budget?

Misusing your debit cards (and make no mistake about it, this is misuse) is the same as misusing cash. But when you run out of cash, you stop spending it. At times, a debit card can be just as bad as a credit card, but instead of paying interest you pay pricey overdraft fees. What's the solution? Make a commitment to discipline. If you are going to enjoy the convenience of a debit card, you should be willing to track every purchase against your budget on a monthly basis. It is nearly impossible to keep a mental note on more than 90 transactions during the course of a month.

On top of the problems you create for yourself via frequent debit card use, your bank can create problems for you as well. As of 2012, many financial institutions have started increasing the fees associated with debit card accounts. In many instances, these institutions are charging between 75 cents and $1.50 every time you enter your debit card PIN (personal identification number). This means every time you withdraw money out of the ATM or every time you enter your PIN to purchase something at a store, you are creating a fee. You can easily rack up $50 per month in these silly fees if you have a debit card usage-frequency issue.

I still believe utilizing a debit card is the best choice, despite the problems it can cause. If you can curtail the mistakes and not get addicted to swiping it, then your debit card can provide the perfect combination of convenience and practicality.

SHOULD YOU SELECT DEBIT OR CREDIT WHEN SWIPING YOUR DEBIT CARD?

I'm sure you've noticed that you can often choose whether to run your debit card as a credit card or a debit card. Have you wondered what the difference is? Here's what happens when you run your debit card as a debit, and here's what happens when you run your debit card as a credit card. In the spirit of full disclosure, I almost always select debit because I think it's fairer to the merchant, and I don't like having a delay in payment processing.

Running as debit:

- ▶ Doing so requires you type in your four-digit PIN.
- ▶ It's the only way to get cash back with no ATM fees.
- ▶ From a merchant's perspective, this is the closest you can get to paying with cash.
- ▶ Fees are minimal to a merchant, and it benefits them for you to use this option. These transactions are considered "online," and your purchase will automatically be deducted from your account.

- ▶ Because these transactions are run through STAR or NYCE, they aren't offered the extra protection of a credit card, though your bank protects all funds in your checking account.

- ▶ In a few rare cases, banks limit debit transactions per month or you are charged fees for using debit. Why? You'll see in the next section.

Running debit as credit:

- ▶ Considered an "offline" purchase, transactions run this way most likely won't come out of your account immediately, but will be charged in a batch in the evening when the store closes, though this varies by merchant.

- ▶ Banks especially benefit from debit cards used as credit because the merchant is charged higher fees that go directly to the bank. This is actually a huge source of revenue for the bank.

- ▶ Because banks benefit from you running your debit card as credit, they will often offer rewards or incentives for choosing this method.

- ▶ You'll notice your debit card has the Visa or MasterCard logo on it. This means when your debit card is run as credit, it is backed by this company. For example, if your debit card is backed by Visa, you are eligible for their zero-liability policy.

- ▶ To cover the high fees charged to the merchant, those fees are often passed back to you, the consumer, in the form of higher prices and/or minimum purchase limits for paying with plastic.

HOW DO YOU ACTUALLY REDUCE SPENDING?

Some people may define financial progress as "being able to afford more." I define it differently, as "needing less money to live."

The fewer financial obligations you have, the more freedom you have. Yet, in part due to the influence of marketing and the media, Americans tend to add obligations as they increase their income and their wealth. If you measure your success by what you have, you're in deep trouble. This isn't cause for panic, though, because you can adjust this attitude. Your spending habits, no matter how deep-seated they are, can change. They *must* change, especially if they are the roadblocks standing in the way of your financial progress.

Not only do you need to change your current "fixed" spending habits, you also must reduce the number of financial obligations you have and those you continue to accept. By making some subtle changes that will have a major impact on your bottom line, you can easily reclaim thousands of dollars per year from your budget.

The following four spending categories can immediately reflect your growing financial awareness (or lack thereof):

▶ Groceries

▶ Dining out

▶ Utilities

▶ The new necessities

GROCERIES

The grocery store is a microcosm of your world when it comes to spending decisions. In this microcosm, you can isolate certain behaviors and decision-making processes, analyze them, and then use the resulting data to alter your financial behaviors in all spending situations.

Do you make impulsive purchases or stick to your grocery list? Are you easily distracted by shiny and sparkly items? These are the type of questions you will consider when analyzing your grocery-store habits.

Good decisions at the grocery store can benefit you in two ways.

▶ They can directly and positively affect your finances in specific areas of your life.

  ▶ By planning meals based on what's on sale and in season, you can reduce your impulse buying, overspending, and food waste. Buying in season and local reduces food transportation costs, thus reducing your cost.

  ▶ You can decrease your healthcare costs by making proper food choices.

  ▶ If you can become immune to catchy but often meaningless grocery-store marketing tactics (such as flashy packaging and strategic shelf placement), you can apply the same discretion to other such tactics that appeal more to your senses than to your needs.

▶ They can help you develop the following good habits, which will carry over to all financial decisions:

  ▶ Frugality

  ▶ Willpower

  ▶ Strategic planning and execution

  ▶ Prioritizing

  ▶ Budgeting and problem solving

If it seems like I'm putting a lot of pressure on your trip to the grocery store, that's because I am. Whereas you've no doubt come to consider these trips a means of picking up food for dinner, I'm focused on the part they play in a much grander financial plan.

Think about it. When you walk through a grocery store, one particular concept is abundantly clear: choice. You could buy anything you want, but should you? You could look for deals, but will your desire for instant gratification trump your need for a good bargain? You could buy brand names, but generic is cheaper and not very different (if at all) from brand-name items. You get to choose how much your compulsions will cost you and how much money you need for instant gratification.

DINING OUT

Not only is dining out convenient, it's fun. No shopping for hard-to-find ingredients, no lengthy preparation, and perhaps best of all, no cleanup.

Unfortunately, if you don't have a grasp on how dining out affects your financial life, you could be in for a great deal of trouble long after you pay the bill.

Sixty-six percent of American adults say they dine in a restaurant at least once a week. A statistic like this one no doubt results in large part from our hectic work schedules. If you're a member of the great American rat race like I am, sometimes you simply don't have the time or the energy to go grocery shopping and prepare adequate meals. On the other hand, if you're working incredibly long hours to sustain your indulgent dining habits, then you might be in the middle of a nasty cycle. (If you're just a workaholic, that's a completely different issue altogether.)

Yet to many, dining out is not only a source of sustenance, it's a primary source of entertainment. Both of these situations are common and fair. But no matter how you look at it, you should be fully aware of how dining out affects your personal bottom line.

The absolute best way to curb your spending on dining out is to track it on a weekly basis. This means giving yourself a weekly dining-out budget. Whether it's $75 or $20, it's much easier to keep track of the 21 meals in a week than it is to keep track of the 93 meals in a month.

UTILITIES

You can apply the same discipline you develop in other areas of your financial life to reducing your utility expenses. The average American has upwards of six or seven fixed expenses each month, including utility bills. But how much attention do you give your utility bills each month?

If you're like most Americans, probably not much. We tend to take the cost of "fixed" bills like these for granted. But are utility bills really fixed? Not really. Your habits, knowledge, and overall awareness can affect them, and you can reduce your utility costs with very little effort. So what do you say? Would you tweak a couple of your habits if it meant freeing up $300 per year? I thought you would.

Take the time to explore the various money-saving programs your different utility providers offer (but which they may not always go out of their way to advertise). For instance, can you bundle your different services? Can you switch to budget billing to avoid seasonal spikes on your bill?

Familiarize yourself with your utility providers' different payment options, either by calling the companies or by visiting their websites. Compare those options to the amount you pay monthly. Are you spending more than necessary to get the services you need? If so, make changes if doing so will ultimately save you money, and then watch the savings happen over the next few months.

You need to manage your utility bills in the same way you manage your assets. Because changing your financial life is all about changing your habits, adopt the following money-saving and energy-saving habits:

▶ **Consider installing a programmable thermostat.** This allows you to be energy efficient when you're away from your home during the day. If you don't have a programmable thermostat, settle on a temperature a few degrees lower (during winter) and higher (during summer) than you're used to. You'll be surprised by how much you can save.

▶ **Turn off your lights when you leave a room.** This is such an easy and obvious way to conserve energy and save money—yet few people do it. There's no need to keep lights on in unoccupied rooms, and there's really no reason to light your front lawn or backyard at night. If you're concerned about intruders or safety, consider switching to motion-detecting lights, which can lead to significant savings over time.

▶ **Conserve water.** Even if your water company doesn't offer an incentive to adopt water-conservation strategies, the potential savings should be incentive enough. Switching to low-flow shower heads and aerated faucets and adding "float boosters" to your toilet tank are great ways for homeowners to lower their water bills.

▶ **Unplug appliances and other devices that use energy when not in use.** This includes your television, toaster, cell-phone charger, and hair dryer. Also, turn off surge protectors and power strips when you're not using the electronics plugged into them. Keeping these items plugged in wastes energy and money.

▶ **Evaluate your need for a home phone.** Sometimes a cell phone can replace a traditional one entirely. Many people no longer need a landline but keep it because they don't want to get rid of a phone number they've had for years. But paying the phone company a fixed amount every month simply for the privilege of having a sentimental phone number and a service you can live without is a lot more painful than the steps you can take to replace your home phone with your cell phone once and for all. If you already have a cell phone and are ready to make the switch, start by emailing your contacts your new number. Next, put your cell phone number on your landline voicemail or answering machine for a month prior to turning off your home phone service. Finally, personally call those you want to have your new number (and skip those you don't!).

▶ **Check for air leaks around windows, doors, seal cracks, and drafty spaces.** Why spend time and money heating or air conditioning your home if the air is escaping? The principle of preventing waste alone should motivate you to investigate your home's efficiency. The principle of saving money is icing on the cake.

These steps may seem minor, but the small things truly do have the largest effects. In my experience, making these changes can save you as much as $300 per year, which you can put toward real financial priorities.

Gabe's story clearly illustrates how these tactics can save money. Gabe, a school counselor and summertime landscaper, always had budgeting problems. During the winter, his problem was particularly pronounced: Heating costs stretched his paycheck so thin that he was constantly hit with overdraft charges. Because one of his jobs was seasonal, his income was higher during the summer (and his heating bills were obviously lower as well). So his real issue wasn't budgeting, but timing—and awareness. He admitted he had never taken the time to consider how his utility bills could be affected by his habits and decisions—he had just come to accept high heating bills in winter as a fact of life.

The solution? He took five minutes to contact his natural gas provider and sign up for their budget-billing program. The program, which spreads heating costs over the entire year's bills, allowed him to pay a consistent amount each month. Instead of having his bill fluctuate between $50 and $400 each month, depending on the season, he paid a fixed fee of $150 per month. This fixed bill didn't eliminate any of Gabe's debt per se, but it did make it easier for him to budget year-round, which drastically improved his ability to focus on his financial goals and the other areas of his budget that needed attention.

THE NEW NECESSITIES

Without a real grasp of their traditional costs (such as utilities)—the majority of Americans have begun justifying the addition of new fixed expenses as well. I'm not going to make the case for getting rid of things you consider necessities—although you should certainly consider it if you're in debt—but they can add up and drain your checking account if each expense isn't monitored carefully. Perhaps the first question you should ask yourself is whether all of your necessities are, in fact, necessities.

Chances are, you have a greater number of "basic life necessities" than you did 10 or 20 years ago—and your list of basic "needs" is probably drastically larger than that of your parents. This is due to what I call the *Simplicity-Needs Paradox*, the contradiction presented when, in taking steps to simplify your life by decreasing the amount of energy you expend on routine tasks, you increase the number of basic needs necessary to maintain your new level of simplicity.

For example, email is far faster than snail mail, but to have access to email, you have to have a computer. Thus, to simplify you have to acquire. As you simplify your financial life, you'll have to account for the new necessities that have become basic needs. But with so many new necessities, how are you ever going to free up enough money to start saving? The basic fact of the matter is, you can't start saving until you stop spending.

Easier said than done, right?

So where can you cut back? The following questions will help you take a bite out of unnecessary spending. Answer the questions, and you'll likely find that you can free up at least $70 per month.

▶ Do you really need the fastest Internet service available? Is there a cheaper plan? Is there a way to consolidate the services you now get into one lower monthly plan? Assuming I'm not driving you back into the Dark Ages of dial-up, which I wouldn't wish upon anyone, write down the potential monthly savings.

▶ Do you even watch your premium cable channels? I didn't, so I opted for the lesser package. You might also be able to unsubscribe from certain channels à la carte, which can also reduce your monthly costs. What does the package one tier below yours cost?

▶ Do you regularly buy frou-frou coffee drinks? How much would you save if you switched to normal coffee and then doctored it with milk and sugar?

▶ Music and movies can be an addiction, but that doesn't mean you have to buy/download them. (No, this isn't where I tell you how to steal it.) Instead, you can go to most libraries and get CDs and DVDs to listen to before you buy. This way you can eliminate the cost of the ones you don't like or get your fix and save your dough. Seriously consider this. Even more, consider how much it would save you.

▶ I like overstuffed burritos, too, but there's no reason you can't cut your lunch budget in half. Make a sandwich, keep salad fixings in the fridge at work—just keep the spending at bay. How much money per month can you take off of your lunch spending?

▶ How can you reduce the cost of your cell phone plan? What about the monthly text-message package or the number of monthly minutes? Can you feasibly move to the usage plan a step below your current one? Some cell phone service companies will actually sit on the phone with you to help you create a more affordable plan. But you have to be proactive and request help— they usually don't advertise this service. How much money can you save with just a couple of small changes to your cell phone plan?

To determine how much you could save monthly on the new necessities, add up the monthly totals you determined from answering the preceding questions. Write that number down. There you go. You may have just created margin.

Andrea, a fortysomething single mother, committed to these steps and managed to save $190 per month. She changed her cable plan, reduced the money she spent on lunch during the workweek, and analyzed her cell phone plan to identify every single area where she could save.

Andrea is a good example of somebody who was wasting a fair amount of money on things she really didn't need (but thought she needed). She didn't cancel her cable; she simply re-evaluated her viewing habits and acted accordingly. She didn't discontinue her cell phone service or even limit her usage; she just discovered that she only used 68 percent of the minutes she purchased each month and thus changed plans to take advantage of the savings that come with her level of usage. (The ratio of cell phone usage to rate plan is one that most of us could stand to lower.) And Andrea's story gets even better: She was ultimately able to put all of her newly "found" money—$2,280 per year, to be exact—toward her son's college fund!

IS IT EVER OKAY TO SPLURGE?

All of this financial restraint can build up some really strange feelings. You may be tempted to blow money.

Whereas being financially responsible can be addicting, sometimes you just want to spend money. It's important to acknowledge this desire and learn how to deal with it. Frankly, sometimes it's okay to splurge. You just need to set some ground rules to prevent the splurge from turning into a disaster.

▶ **Don't splurge to make yourself feel better about a bad financial situation.** Splurging in the midst of financial struggles is a bad idea. Once the high wears off from the splurge, reality will be all up in your face. A good way to splurge when you are broke is to splurge with another resource: time. Take the day to yourself. Go to a park and walk around. Go walk around the mall (but don't splurge). Just collect your thoughts and enjoy the silence. (It's quite obvious at this point that I have a toddler, isn't it?)

▶ **Plan your splurges.** Yes, I know I'm taking a bit of the fun out of it. That's just what I do. Splurge once per quarter (every three months). And better yet, plan your splurges by reducing spending in other categories leading up to the big splurge.

▶ **Don't be a fool.** Yep, that's the type of hard-hitting advice you can only get from Pete the Planner. Splurging on a car is a bad idea. Splurging on a time-share is a bad idea. Splurge on dinner. Splurge on a sweater. Splurge on a gift for your significant other.

Life isn't all about restriction. Your ability to splurge responsibly will serve you well. Yes, planning your splurge is the right thing to do. Don't make this the worst advice I have ever given; please splurge responsibly.

CHAPTER 4

THE PIE: BUDGETING

I'm a realist. I know that it's quite likely you've made it to this point in your life without actively budgeting. And your solvency may convince you that budgeting was never necessary, and it won't be necessary for you to remain solvent and financially viable. If I agree to understand these feeling you might possess, I'd ask that you extend an understanding to me as a courtesy. Here's what I need you to understand: It's best that you don't wait to change your eating habits until after a heart attack.

You probably have about 20 years left in your career. This means you have 20 years left of earned income. This earned income must eliminate your debts, fund your present lifestyle, and fund your life post-work. And if you're like many people in their forties, your current demands for money via your present lifestyle have been screaming for your income louder than your past obligations and your future plans have.

If nothing else, your money life in your forties needs focus. I hate to be the bearer of good news, but your focus will come in the form of a pie chart. Yep, your budget.

How else will you know if you are spending too much on entertainment? How are you possibly to know if all that money you are spending on travel soccer for little Davey is too much? And finally, how are you to know if you're addicted to your income? Yes, addicted to your income…

Your forties should be the beginning of your quest for income independence. You've heard the term *financial independence* several times. But it's unlikely you've considered, or even heard of, *income independence*. Income independence is the idea and practice of eliminating your monthly financial obligations to become less dependent on your income. For instance, if you consistently save 30 percent of your income, gross or net, then you're consistently dependent on only 70 percent of your income. If you save 0 percent of your income, then you are desperately dependent on 100 percent of your income.

Don't dismiss this idea as simplistic. It isn't. Well, it kinda is. Yes, it is. Why should retirement planning be anymore complicated than that? You know how much stuff you have going on in your life right now. Do you really have the energy, patience, or focus for anything more complicated than attacking retirement by eliminating your desperate need for copious amounts of income? Me neither.

Your budget is the key to not only sorting out the complicated nature of your current life, but also allowing you to retire with grace and a confident aura of income independence.

It seems like you should naturally know how to budget. You calculate your income, determine your spending on various expense categories, and then try to spend less than your income provides. But it's just not that simple. Budgeting isn't organic. Budgeting doesn't spontaneously occur. It's a challenging activity that doesn't happen until you decide that it needs to be an important part of your financial life.

And you will eventually get to this point. You will eventually decide that having a budget will enhance your financial life. You can put off this decision for as long as you like, but you will, in the end, budget. A day doesn't go by that a new retiree isn't forced to budget for the first time. Fixed income and fixed expenses always force this decision. Teaching a 65-year-old how to budget can be very challenging. When you operate your entire adult life without a budget for roughly 40 years, being forced to budget becomes a matter of financial survival.

Many fortysomethings, on the other hand, don't budget because they are overconfident in their ability to earn more and more income. We have become accustomed to constantly increasing incomes. We assume that our incomes will increase with age. This isn't true. U.S. Census Bureau statistics show that the U.S. median household income fell 2.9 percent in 2009. Of even greater concern is the fact that average annual expenditures per consumer unit fell 2.8 percent in 2009, following an increase of 1.7 percent in 2008. This means that income fell more than consumer spending fell. America was still overspending during the most financially devastating time in recent history.

Your income is not guaranteed to increase. Your subliminal excuse for not budgeting is bogus. You must budget. But this is where things get tricky. The word "budget" is used to describe several different types of activities and processes. Let's examine these.

▶ **Budget (noun).** This word isn't as straightforward as you think. "Budget" can be used to describe anticipated spending, or it can be used to describe a comparison of your income and expenses. The difference often stops people before they get started. My first "budget" was a single snapshot of my expected expenses. But it stopped there. Stopping at the one-time snapshot is a very common yet troublesome mistake.

▶ **Budget (verb).** The actual possession or completion of a budget is not sufficient. To actually accomplish something, you must actively budget. Consistent attention to budgeting will lead to lifelong financial success. This isn't as tedious as it may seem. If you are willing to dedicate 20 minutes per month to your finances, then you have a chance of living relatively stress-free.

IS IT TIME TO RELENT?

There are constant signs in your financial life that indicate you should be budgeting. These signs often appear in the form of financial adversity. If any of these things has happened to you, then it's time to get serious and start budgeting.

▶ Overdraft charges at your bank

▶ Credit card debt

▶ Financial stress

▶ Relationship problems regarding money

▶ Daily visits to your online banking account

▶ Personal debts to a family member or friend

You can either ignore these signs—which will eventually bring you back to the original predicament—or take stock now.

Somehow when random negative financial events occur, people tend to flip out. We know emergencies are going to occur; yet we're rarely prepared for them financially. Worse, people often look for someone else to blame when financial turmoil arises.

Consistent budgeting can prevent this manufactured feeling of helplessness.

About once a year every year, I meet people who are shocked to have to come up with some cash to replace the brakes on their car. They are incredibly surprised, as though they'd awoken that morning with their heads sewn to their pillows. As far as I know, no set of brakes lasts forever. So, our lack of preparation for this moment is our fault. And if this sort of "emergency" tends to occur over and over again, it's time to change. Financial mistakes don't appear in the emergency—they appear in the aftermath. If you don't change your behavior, then you consistently will get the same undesired result.

THE IDEAL HOUSEHOLD BUDGET

The most frequently asked question I get about budgeting is, "How much money should I be spending on each expense category?" Good news: I have an answer for that. It's called the *ideal household budget*.

Don't panic if your expenses don't look exactly like this chart. The key to this entire exercise is to make sure your pie actually equals 100 percent. Yes, in doing this you may find that you spend more money than you make, but we will fix that problem by the end of this book.

Here is what you need to know: If you don't spend the maximum amount in one category, you can allocate more money to another category. In other words, let's say that your household

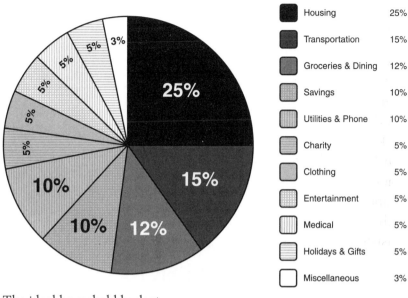

■ Housing	25%
■ Transportation	15%
■ Groceries & Dining	12%
■ Savings	10%
■ Utilities & Phone	10%
■ Charity	5%
■ Clothing	5%
■ Entertainment	5%
■ Medical	5%
■ Holidays & Gifts	5%
□ Miscellaneous	3%

The ideal household budget.

transportation costs are only 5 percent of your income. Then you can feel comfortable allocating the "extra" 10 percent to other categories. This strategy is exactly how I live the financial life I want to live. I have very low transportation costs; therefore, dining out and housing receive a higher portion of my income. In addition, I don't spend much on entertainment or medical care; therefore, I'm able to utilize these allocations elsewhere. See? It's kind of fun.

People who fail to operate on this give-and-take basis often find themselves in debt. Many households operate on 110 percent of their income. You just can't do that. You can't consistently spend more than you make and expect to come out on the other end. I encourage you to compare your household expenditures to this chart and this philosophy. What one category do you scrimp on so that you can spend more on another?

You'll notice the ideal household budget excludes employer-sponsored retirement plan deposits, such as a 401(k). There's a simple explanation for that. Employer-sponsored retirement plan deposits are often taken out of your income prior to it being considered take-home pay. Thus, if you save 15 percent of your gross income toward your 401(k) and another 10 percent of your take-home pay toward general savings, you are a rock star. Check that—a rock star probably wouldn't save any money.

RENT/MORTGAGE, INCLUDING PROPERTY TAXES AND PROPERTY INSURANCE: 25 PERCENT

Your housing expense is generally your largest one. This means that poor decisions with regard to housing can have a long-lasting impact on your financial life.

Banks have traditionally allowed mortgage payments to approach 33 percent of a gross monthly income (before taxes). That's not at all surprising; a bank is in business to make money first and help you second (or third...or fourth...don't get me started). Thirty-three percent of gross is very different from 25 percent of net. For instance, if your household income is $70,000, 33 percent of your gross monthly income would be $1,924 ($70,000 / 12 = $5,833, and $5,833 × 33% = $1,924). In contrast, 25 percent of your net income on $70,000 would be approximately $1,020, based on $49,000 take-home pay ($70,000 × 70% (30% for taxes and benefits) = $49,000, and $49,000 / 12 = $4,083. $4,083 × 25% = $1,020). That is a difference of $904 per month! I don't know about you, but I spend my net income, not my gross income.

You immediately back yourself into a corner when you commit too much of your income to housing. Based on where you live geographically, it may be easier to keep your housing spending in check. But even if you live in an expensive area for housing, such as San Francisco or Manhattan, knowing your limits is key.

TRANSPORTATION: 15 PERCENT

Do you drive your car? Or does your car drive you...to financial trouble? If you're fortunate enough to live in an area with good public transportation, then you're lucky, and you're likely to spend much less on transportation than those people who are forced to rely on personal transportation options..

For the rest of us, getting to the places we need to go costs money. Historically, Americans have moved farther and farther away from our places of employment and have consistently increased the length of our car loans. You might not think so, but living 20 miles away from your job with an eight-year car loan could lead to your financial ruin.

I once encountered a woman who spent 54 percent of her income on transportation. She was in a rough financial situation excluding transportation, and when you threw transportation into the mix, her financial life was a disaster. She spent a majority of the money she earned just to get to her job. She finally relented, gave up being a car owner for eight months, took the bus, and got her financial life back in order.

Car lending has some of the loosest restrictions in the debt marketplace. And allowing a lender or car dealer to dictate the affordability of a certain vehicle will lead to major financial problems.

Transportation costs typically include car payments (leases or loans), gas, insurance, and maintenance. It is very easy to let your transportation costs creep above 15 percent of your take-home pay. This should lead you to one conclusion: You need to find a semi-permanent solution to high transportation costs. Pay off your car and settle close to your place of employment. Based on that hypothetical $70,000 income, you should allocate no more than $612 per month to transportation.

There's added complexity to this expense category once you consider the changing nature of our transportation needs. Our lifestyles impact what type of vehicles we drive. When on our own, we could justify driving a one-seater car, if such a vehicle existed. But if our family structure changes, then so must our transportation decisions. That motorcycle gets turned in for a sedan, and then the sedan gets turned in for—wait for it!—a minivan. The minivan goes away eventually, but then it's replaced by a third and maybe even a fourth car as teen drivers enter the mix.

If you have a teen driver, the cost of your auto insurance will be much more than you really want to pay for it. How are you going to react? Are you going to try to absorb the increased expenses? Or are you going to cut your spending in other categories? The answer should be to cut expenses in other categories. But what categories? Saving? Let's hope not.

When your transportation needs change, you can't try to rationalize a poor financial decision by summoning the "it's for the family" defense. Making sacrifices for the good of your family is admirable, but sacrificing the financial security of your family in an effort to sacrifice *for* your family is as counterproductive as it is common. And it's pretty darn common.

GROCERIES AND DINING OUT: 12 PERCENT

Humans have an odd relationship with food, so much so that we often express our love of food with one of our most precious resources—money. Your money and your consumption of food can at times be overwhelming. I've seen typical families spend upwards of $1,800 per month on food. I've seen financial lives ruined by food, and I once saw a couple blow through 12 percent of their retirement assets in the first year of retirement because they spent so much money on food.

So what is a person supposed to spend on food? And at what point does your food-spending equal a problem?

According to the ideal household budget, it is reasonable to spend 12 percent of your net (after-tax) household income on food. That number includes groceries, dining out, coffee, fermented beverages, and anything else your mouth might consume. For instance, if your take-home pay is $4,000 per month, then your food budget is $480 per month. Is that reasonable? Maybe. But honestly, the 12 percent is a guide. If you spend more than 12 percent of your income on food, then you need to rob some other area of your life to pay for it. What's it gonna be? Your transportation budget? Your savings? Your clothing budget? I don't really care what other area of your financial life you choose to short, but you must account for each and every percentage point that climbs over 12 percent.

People overindulge with food for one of three reasons. First, there's convenience. Any time you exchange money for time, that's convenience. If you are driving home from your kid's soccer practice and you don't want to take the time to make dinner when you get home, then you must exchange money for convenience. Don't want to wake up five minutes earlier to pack your lunch for work? Cool. Just know you'll need to exchange money for convenience. And if you exchange money for time too often, you'll have a big financial problem.

The second reason people struggle with their food budget is because some people view food and beverage as entertainment. For transparency's sake, this is me. While I sometimes spend too much money on food because of a desire for convenience, I often find that my food overspending is a product of my desire to be entertained by food. I find a delicious meal prepared by a trained chef to be as entertaining as a concert or a movie. And this is specifically why I move the 5 percent that's allocated to entertainment in my ideal household budget toward food. In other words, I spend 17 percent of my income on food. I obviously surpass the prescribed 12 percent, but I account for this by eliminating my entertainment. Besides, I have two toddlers. Entertainment for me is silence.

The third reason people overspend on food is a bit more intricate. I've found that some people are so health conscious that they will buy only organic and specialty foods. While focusing on a healthy lifestyle is certainly a brilliant idea, destroying your finances in the process is a terrible idea. This is why people with a health-food issue should reallocate the 5 percent that's designated for health and medical in the ideal household budget toward food. But if a person with a health-food overspending issue also has other medical expenses, then more expense categories will need to be reduced. Sometimes our health issues require us to spend more money on food. If this is the case for you, just make sure you find the extra money you need to spend on food somewhere else in your budget.

We want it all. The real problems I see often involve people who want convenience, gourmet food, and the healthiest ingredients on the planet. Idealistically, good for them. Realistically, they are going to have a major financial issue that spans years. Food, although a huge part of our lives and culture, is fleeting. We consume it. It leaves our bodies. And as crass as that might seem, your money might just turn into waste.

As your family grows, so will your grocery expenses. This can sneak up on you. What starts out as maybe a baby formula expense and some rice cereal can quickly turn into several extra gallons of milk per week and growing children with bottomless pits for stomachs. You have to keep an eye on this. As your food expenses increase, you must make sure that you reallocate dollars away from another expense category. Ideally, that other expense category won't be your savings.

SAVINGS: 10 PERCENT

Not only should you save money in a company-sponsored retirement plan prior to your paycheck hitting your checking account, but you should also save 10 percent of your take-home pay. This isn't hard to do if you build the habit from your first paycheck. But the further away you get from your first paycheck, the harder it gets. And if you're in your forties, there's a solid chance you are pretty far removed from your first paycheck. You might want to start with 5 percent and creep yourself up to 10 percent over a period of three months or so.

Consistently save 10 percent of your income until your emergency fund (three months' worth of expenses) is full, and then start putting your 10 percent savings toward your middle bucket. We'll discuss the middle bucket at length in Chapter 7, "The Piggy Bank: Saving and Investing."

If you have consumer debt, then the 10 percent allocated to savings should actually go toward debt reduction. From a net-worth perspective, which you'll learn more about in Chapter 7, paying down debt and saving money are the same things. Don't feel pressure to put money in your emergency fund while you're focusing on paying off debt. You can get away with $1,000 or so in your emergency fund while you aggressively attack credit card debt and the like.

Whereas at first this 10 percent allocation will go to vanquish debt and build your emergency fund, at some point it will transition into tasks such as college funding and other forms of investing.

UTILITIES: 10 PERCENT

Utilities are utilities, but that doesn't mean you can't help yourself out when making important spending decisions. Internet access, smartphones, and data plans have changed the boring world of utility bills forever. Our addictions to these new types of utility payments have channeled money away from our savings and investments. Anecdotally, it's not uncommon for people to pay more for their smartphone data plan than they save for their child's education.

But it's not just the newfangled utility bills that challenge. Our utility bills don't just happen to us; we sign up for them. Often, our utility costs become more than we want them to be when we buy too much house—the side effect of buying too much house is high utility bills. If you made your housing decision during a string of thriving months and have now come back down to a more modest income level, then not only will your mortgage payment continue to be difficult, but the utility payments that support your home will be difficult, too.

As your family dynamic changes, so will your utility bills. That's primarily because of the number of people using smartphone data plans in your household. I get it. I know that we're all tethered to our smartphones. But again, if you're going to spend upwards of $200 per month on smartphone usage, then you must sacrifice some other habit to the tune of $2,400 or more per year.

CHARITY: 5 PERCENT

Your community will only be as good as your commitment to it. If all of your financial resources are used for your household alone, your community will suffer. When your community suffers, you will suffer. Including charity in a budget is difficult for anyone, but it is important for everyone.

Who said charity costs money? A charitable spirit starts in your mind, not in your wallet. If you are waiting to have money before you give, then you will never give. Money is not the determining factor for whether you give; your charitable spirit is. Volunteer, start a canned-food drive, or give stuff you don't use to a charitable organization. Don't just sit there and do nothing. You have two primary economic resources, time and money. When money can't participate, bring your time to the table.

If you're a parent, you'd probably agree that it's in everyone's best interests if you passed on your charitable spirit to the next generation. It's kind of hard for a kid to hear one thing and see another. Your charitable actions speak much louder than words.

CLOTHING: 5 PERCENT

What's included in the clothing budget?

Everything. Clothes for you. Clothes for your kids. Clothes for your spouse. Workout clothes. Work clothes. Casual clothes. Bridesmaid dresses. Rental tuxes. Dry cleaning. Clothing repairs. Shoes. Handbags. More shoes.

You may have been excited by the raw numbers, but the "what's included" section may have brought you back to earth. This requires planning and forethought. The first step, in my opinion? You *must* take care of your current clothing.

Your forties also mark a time in which you may be spending an inordinate amount of money on your children's clothes. Your kids' consumer habits will be formed even when shopping for clothes. You can choose to either set the tone or be a less-than-innocent bystander.

The bottom line is that you should plan your clothing purchases. If you need to spend more than 5 percent of your take-home pay, then cool. Just spend less in some other budget category.

MEDICAL: 5 PERCENT

If your health-insurance premiums are deducted from the paycheck you receive from your employer pre-tax, then the 5 percent allocated to medical expenses in the ideal household budget will likely be limited to co-pays, prescription-drug costs, and fitness memberships. If you pay for your health insurance *with* your take-home pay, then this 5 percent allocation must be used for your health-insurance premiums, too. In fact, it's unlikely you'll be able to jam your health-care expenses into 5 percent of your take-home pay if that's the case.

ENTERTAINMENT: 5 PERCENT

Not to suggest that enjoying life isn't important, because it is, but your entertainment expense category should truly form itself around your financial life. If money is tight, stability is nowhere to be found, and ends aren't meeting, then you really shouldn't be spending much money on entertaining yourself—or your children, for that matter. It's not unusual for financially unstable people to spend a tremendous amount of money on their children's entertainment, while their financial life is crumbling.

If your family structure is changing, keep your eye on this category. From youth travel sports to zoo memberships, your forties can create some new entertainment expenses very quickly.

The entertainment expense category includes travel, hobbies, or any other expense that is pleasure-driven. Again, the absence of pleasure isn't the goal; the goal is satisfaction. And satisfaction is deeper than the shallow ilk of pleasure-driven instant gratification.

HOLIDAYS AND GIFTS: 5 PERCENT

Do you want to waste opportunity wrapped in a bow? Blow through your entire margin during the holidays. It happens all the time. The timing of your end-of-the-year bonus isn't a Christmas miracle; it's an arbitrary coincidence created thousands of years ago when humanity needed a calendar. It's easy to trick yourself into thinking that when you're spending money on someone else, it's a justifiable, benevolent decision. It may be, but that's unlikely. If you're spending money on gifts for your immediate family, you're spending money on yourself.

MISCELLANEOUS: 3 PERCENT

The dreaded, mysterious, and foggy miscellaneous spending category can ruin your financial life. Why? Because these are your whims. This is discretionary beyond discretion. You will have miscellaneous expenses, but disorganized, unaccountable people tend to have a ton of miscellaneous expenses.

There are some very legitimate expenses in this category that many reasonable and responsible people will have. The miscellaneous category is your home for life-insurance premiums, disability-insurance premiums, pet expenses, and household items. But if you have a "stop at Target or Walmart on the way home every day" problem, not only will your entire budget suffer, but your miscellaneous budget will also get destroyed.

THE EXPENSE CATEGORIES YOU DON'T SEE

You probably noticed that some very common expenses weren't part of the ideal household budget. Well, lots of expenses aren't part of the ideal household budget. That's not only okay, it's on purpose. Everyone has expenses that don't fall neatly into line with this pie chart. Your challenge is to make room for these other expenses by reducing your spending in the main categories.

As silly as this is to both write and hear, you shouldn't spend more than 100 percent of your take-home pay. However, it's easier said than done. There are many reasons for this, but spending one's gross income is among the biggest culprits. I've found that people often view their income pre-tax and spend it accordingly. For instance, "I make $100,000 per year; of course I can afford a $500 per month car payment." But our gross incomes have very little to do with our net incomes. Based on the amount of deductions you may have, your take-home (net) pay may be only $4,000 per month—not the $8,333.33 per month that we often convince ourselves $100,000 per year gross generates.

STUDENT LOANS

The clock is ticking. Finish what you started. The longer student loans hang around, the more inconveniences they can cause. Resolve to pay them off. You cannot, under any circumstances, carry student loan debt into your fifties.

EDUCATION

Whether you're dealing with your education expenses or someone else's, you need to make room in your household budget. If you have significant monthly education expenses, you will need to significantly reduce your spending in other areas. One of the most common errors I regularly see in this regard is when parents decide to put their children through private school. The problem isn't the cost of private school; the problem is that parents often don't reduce spending to properly afford private school. This is especially dangerous as parents begin to prepare for college expenses.

Making something like education a priority is great, but making something a priority means de-prioritizing other areas of one's life. If education is going to require more of your discretionary income than the other areas of your life, then you must compromise in the areas you valued greatly in the past. You can't all of a sudden spend more money on education without adjusting the rest of your budget. Sadly, I see this happen quite frequently.

Educations—especially college educations—can be funded via cash flow, with debt, or with assets. If you choose to fund education through cash flow, then just make sure you are adjusting the rest of your budget. If you don't, what you thought was cash flow can quickly turn to debt creation.

DEBT REDUCTION

Ask 100 people how they're going to find enough money to get out of debt, and 99 of them will look outside of their budget. Fortunately, you don't have to look outside of your budget. Your opportunity to pay down your debt lives within your budget. If you have debt—especially consumer debt, such as credit cards, medical bills, or home equity lines—then you need to budget in debt reduction. You must make your debt payments, including additional money to pay toward the principal of your lowest-balance debt, part of your household budget. Debt gets paid off when you take it seriously and stop addressing it with whatever's left at the end of your month.

Look at the ideal household budget and commit to spending less on the core expense categories so that you can rid yourself of consumer debt for good.

VACATION

A vacation is a nice way to reset the stress meter, but going on vacation when you financially shouldn't will only cause the stress meter to spin out of control.

There are a few no-nos when it comes to paying for a vacation. First, don't use a credit card to buy your plane tickets and book your hotel room six months out from a vacation, and then try to figure out how you're going to truly afford it. Pre-fund your vacation, but don't do it with a credit card. Secondly, don't use your emergency fund for a vacation. An emergency fund is not a vacation fund. A $5,000 European vacation is not an emergency, no matter how much you want it to be.

If you have children, vacation decisions get a bit murky with the pressures to create memories and experiences for your children. Family experiences and trips are important, but they must be reconciled with financial reality. Putting your family at a significant economic disadvantage under the guise of memory-creation doesn't make much sense.

KIDS

If you become a parent, you find out very early that your financial life will never be the same. From diapers to formula to gymnastics classes, raising a child is very expensive. At least once per year, you should take the time to evaluate how much money you spend on your children versus how much money you invest for your children. This comparison is an admittedly slippery slope. You might call private soccer lessons an investment, while I might call private soccer lessons for your child entertainment.

Again, you can use the term *investing* to justify quite a few bad decisions. Most of the money that is allocated toward your children is likely to be spent, not invested. But as you will see in Chapter 7, "The Piggy Bank: Saving and Investing," investing for your child's future is important, too.

BUT I DO ALL MY SHOPPING AT ONE STORE

Big-box stores have created some interesting challenges for today's consumers. Target, Walmart, Meijer, and the like are great stores that make shopping convenient and nearly effortless. Who doesn't love buying eggs at the same store where you can buy a shotgun or an espresso maker (in Clementine orange)? In other words, you can buy any miscellaneous item with great ease. But when it comes to budgeting, miscellaneous is the bane of human existence. The more miscellaneous expenditures you have, the more challenging budgeting becomes.

And if you think these purchase-all-things-you-could-possibly-need stores are challenging to budget for, consider the problems that warehouse stores such as Sam's Club and Costco can create. How can a person rectify a budget when faced with six months' worth of salad dressing and a 5-liter bottle of high-end vodka? Well, it's tough. But you must account for the changes in retailers' business practices.

Ultimately, you can adjust your budgeting and financial practices to match the changing nature of your buying habits. For instance, consider making your favorite store its own budget category. Do you have a Target problem? Then make Target its own expense category. This category will most likely engulf your grocery budget, clothing, and even part of your holidays and gifts budget. But that's okay. Budgeting can be more effective when you take your buying habits into consideration when creating your budget categories.

You've heard stories (perhaps even from yourself) of entering one of these types of stores for only one item and ending up with $75 worth of stuff in the cart. How does that happen? Why does that happen? Lots of reasons, but it's less of a big deal when you make the store its own budget category.

Let's say you budget $400 per month for Walmart. Your goal should be to know your limits every time you walk into the store. If you go to Walmart twice per week, then just know you should keep your spending to $50 per trip to stay under your $400 monthly budget. If you go to the store that frequently, then you will know what $50 worth of stuff in your cart looks like.

This is exactly why I go to the same grocery store every week. The more stores you go to on a random basis to get the same type of stuff, the more money you will spend. Being a creature of habit can have its advantages, and one of these advantages is having cart awareness. I don't know about you, but I can look down in my grocery cart and guess the cost of all the groceries within five bucks or so.

The alternative, you ask? The alternative is taking home every receipt, breaking down each item into each budget category, and subsequently ripping all of your hair out as you abandon budgeting forever. My goal for you is to prevent you from giving up on budgeting out of frustration and tediousness. Making your favorite store a budget category will prevent this from happening.

HOW DO YOUR EXPENSES STACK UP?

It's time to put pen to paper. Now that you know what an ideal household budget looks like, you need to take a moment to see how your spending compares. It might be pretty or it might be ugly. Either way, you need to do it.

If your expenses look great next to the ideal household budget, use this opportunity to push yourself even further toward financial wellness. If your expenses look terrible next to the ideal household budget, don't bury your head in the sand and ignore reality.

Your goal in either instance is to identify a chunk of money that you can consistently commit to your financial priorities every month. Chapter 9, "The Plan," will give you the exact action plan for when and how to use this chunk of money. Your goal is just to find it for now.

CHAPTER 5

THE POSSESSIONS: MAJOR PURCHASES

Your ability to set goals to buy a house, a car, or any other major purchase must match with an ability to show restraint and wisdom. If you let others dictate what you can afford, you will grow to regret your purchases.

You must own the "can I afford it" conversation. You must do your own calculations. And you mustn't blindly push the envelope of affordability in any major purchase decision. A mortgage bank isn't the only institution that will let you borrow more than you should; so will a car dealership and a college admissions office.

Because most people's largest purchase in their life is their home, we'll start there.

HOUSING

For most people, a house is the biggest purchase they will ever make. It often commits people to pay hundreds of thousands of dollars for the home and tens of thousands (if not hundreds of thousands) of dollars in interest. And it takes three decades to do it!

Being able to keep a housing purchase in its proper perspective is vital to your financial success.

YOUR MONTHLY COMMITMENT

Our natural inclination is to buy as much house as we are allowed, and sadly, that natural inclination is disgustingly cruel. In many ways, it's much like eating at an all-you-can-eat buffet. The foolish part of our bodies, wherever it may be, convinces us that more is better. But it's not. More can be hell. I'd argue that "more is better" has become the American Way. Oddly enough, I believe that more is better, just not in the way you'd think.

What do you want more of? This is an essential question, especially for prospective homeowners. Prospective homeowners generally are thinking about housing when they set out to buy a house. But it's foolish for that to be all they think about. Buying a house is a tremendously big deal. In many instances, it's the single largest purchase you will ever make. Yet it's rarely treated that way. It's quite strange how we got here, but somewhere along the way, our homes became disproportionately important to us.

I probably don't need to explain why our homes are such an emotional entity, but I will. Our homes are the epicenters of our memories. They keep our children safe; they host meals, parties, prom pictures, and goodbyes. In many ways, our lives wouldn't be complete without a place to host our greatest memories. All of those things can happen anywhere, perhaps for much less than you're currently spending. You will taint your ability to create lovely memories if you make a foolish housing decision. You can prevent this by having the proper focus when making a house decision. That focus? Your life.

Your life isn't about shelter, couches, curtains, square footage, basements, three-car garages, or corner lots. Your life is about everything other than your house: food, vacations, education, family, entertainment, and a ton of other stuff. You cannot afford to do any of these things or indulge any of your interests if your house payment is a disproportionate share of your household budget. Consider these benchmark numbers for housing.

- ▶ **40 percent or more of household income committed to housing.** Your margin of error is very slim. You are clinically overhoused. You should seek an immediate solution to this problem, especially if you have a car payment, student-loan debt, and/or other consumer debt. It's nearly impossible to save for the future when this much money is going toward your house payment. It is very unlikely that you have a properly funded emergency fund (three months' worth of expenses).

- ▶ **26 to 39 percent of household income committed to housing.** You listened to the bank, or you followed the advice of a mortgage calculator. You are spending too much on housing, but it's not a fatal error. If you lack a car payment and significant debt, then you should be fine. If you have a car payment or debt, then you are at risk of hating your financial life for a long time.

- ▶ **25 percent of household income committed to housing.** Life is manageable, fruitful, and comfortable when you can limit your house payment to 25 percent of your income. You can get the best of both worlds: a nice home and a nice payment.

▶ **Less than 25 percent of household income committed to housing.** Do you want everything, and are you willing to sacrifice a foolish housing decision to get it? Awesome. Then spend less than 25 percent of your household income on a house payment. Travel the world. Dine out. Drive a sweet ride. Drink copious amounts of craft beer. You can do these things when you don't over-commit to ridiculous housing costs.

Furthermore, if your mortgage or rent payment, combined with your transportation costs (car payment, insurance, gas), is more than 55 percent of your household income, then we've officially figured out why your financial life is so difficult right now.

Show restraint when making a housing decision. You'll actually be able to live a life you want to live.

FIVE SIGNS THAT YOU BOUGHT TOO MUCH HOUSE

One of the most common financial problems facing Americans today is owning too much home. And by *owning*, I mean being in the process of owning—in other words, securing a mortgage for a house in which you can't afford to live. This is a very serious problem. If this happens to be your problem, then you need to address it ASAP. Because foreclosure risk is real for those who can't afford the home in which they live.

What sort of problems can having too much house cause? Well, lots. High utility costs, high maintenance costs, and high stress levels, to name a few. But low housing liquidity and high foreclosure risks are what would keep me up at night. Housing liquidity describes how easy it would be for you to quickly sell your home at an acceptable price. The lower the liquidity, the harder it would be to get rid of your house in an emergency situation (job transfer, budget constraints, and so on). Unfortunately, as you will see in a moment, some of the same signs that illuminate the fact that you can't afford your house also prevent you from selling your house in a prompt manner.

▶ **You have no equity.** How much of your house do you own? Your answer will determine whether you are in a healthy housing situation. Equity, of course, is the amount of ownership you have in something (in this instance, your home). Do you have less than 5 percent ownership of your home? If so, then you are in too much home. What? The market fell and ate up your ownership? Yes, that stinks, but you still are in too much home. Low equity equals home-selling difficulty. Remember our brief discussion about housing liquidity? Having home equity can prevent you from having housing-liquidity issues. Low equity isn't the end of the world, but fire is falling from the sky if you have low equity combined with one or two of the following signs.

▶ **Your payment is 40 percent of your monthly income.** The maximum amount of your monthly income that should be dedicated to your mortgage payment is 25 percent. It is quite possible that if your mortgage payment ranges up to 30 to 35 percent of your income, you will still be all right. But if 40 percent of your household income goes to pay your mortgage, then you could be in really big trouble. This isn't always the case, but it is *often* the case. And the more you spend on housing, the less you can spend on everything else!

This means you most likely can't save money, can't pay off debt, and can't go on vacation. It is quite common for people who have a major debt issue to mistake a problem of too much house for a debt problem. Having a high housing cost percentage leaves you very little room for error.

▶ **You can't afford to keep up with yard and house maintenance.** Haven't mulched in two years? Can't afford to paint your house? Those are signs that you can't afford the house in which you live. If you have to go into debt to perform the most basic of home maintenance, then you can't afford your home. The worst part is that neglecting upkeep will only make your problem of too much house worse. Your property value will suffer from your lack of attention. This will increase your housing-liquidity concerns.

▶ **You have unfurnished rooms.** What's the point of having a room that you don't use? There is a ritzy section of the city where I live that is famous for having gigantic homes with no furniture. You don't have to have a perfectly decorated home, but there is something incredibly odd about buying a large home and then not having enough cash flow to furnish it. Right?

▶ **You struggle to afford property tax increases.** I believe it was Henry David Thoreau who once said, "No, I'm not going to pay property taxes." Okay, he may not have said that...but anyway, no one likes paying property taxes. No one. Property taxes will consistently increase either through increased tax rates or through increased property values. Not being able to afford this increase is a major sign that you are in trouble.

If you are guilty of at least three of these issues, then you have a serious problem. Don't take it lightly if you can't afford your current home. That stress you are feeling…yeah, it's real. This problem won't solve itself. But acting in haste will only worsen your problem. I do think that you need to get some professionals involved. You should contact a licensed and trusted realtor to give you an estimate of what your home is worth. You need information. Regardless of whether you sell your home, you need to know where you stand. The solution very well may be that you should sell your home. This is a terribly tough decision, but it could save the rest of your financial life.

So, assuming you aren't going to sell your home, now what? You *must* turn to your budget. Don't know how much you should spend on stuff? Then use the ideal household budget in Chapter 4. If you can't afford your house, then you are likely committing too much of your household income to your mortgage payment. This means you need to either make more money or spend less money. Spoiler alert for the rest of your financial life: Those are always the two options. In some cases you might want to consider getting an additional job. This should help you temporarily increase your income so that you can take another more permanent course of action (such as selling your house).

If you do sell your house, then you are unlikely to have a ton of equity for a down payment on another house. Take this as a sign from God, and don't buy another house. Rent. Renting is not second place. Renting is one of the smartest financial decisions you can make. The crazy thing is that you can probably rent a house in the same neighborhood where you currently live…for less than what you are paying for your mortgage.

I can't emphasize my final point enough: Time won't solve this problem. Only three things solve the problem of having too much house: spending less money, making more money, or selling your house. And in most instances, you need to do all three. Don't be embarrassed, be empowered. You are about to take control of your out-of-control financial life. And don't forget, I'm here to help.

THE KEY TO HOUSING SUCCESS

There was a time when mortgages were four years long. You agreed to buy a house, you moved in, and then you had four years to pay it off. If that was still the standard today, then many of us would be renting and/or living in much less expensive homes. Stretching out the length of time on a mortgage has been the single biggest reason why home-ownership rates skyrocketed through the middle part of the twentieth century. While the 30-year fixed-rate mortgage certainly has become the most common type of mortgage, the 15-year fixed-rate mortgage often makes more sense.

By their nature, 15-year fixed-rate mortgages will always have a lower interest rate than 30-year fixed-rate mortgages. This is just the way that debt and liquidity work. For instance, if you let your bank borrow your money for six months, via a six-month certificate of deposit (CD), they may only pay you 0.5 percent interest. But if you let them borrow your money for five years, via a five-year CD, then they may pay you 2.5 percent. This is because you will have much less liquidity if you have your money locked up for five years. This liquidity, or lack thereof, is the primary factor for being able to charge a higher interest rate.

Let's look at a 30-year mortgage at 4 percent on a $200,000 loan (no taxes and insurance).

Mortgage Repayment Summary	
Loan amount	$200,000
Interest rate	4%
Mortgage term	30 years
Monthly payment	$954.83
Total of 360 payments	$343,739.01
Total interest paid	$143,739.01
Payoff date	July 2044

As you can clearly see, you will have paid $343,739.01 to pay off a $200,000 loan. You will have paid the bank 72 percent more than you borrowed originally if you complete the entire mortgage. But in exchange for this large amount of interest that you will pay, you will have a relatively low monthly payment. And as you will notice in my next example, the low payment isn't a product of anything other than spreading out your repayment over 30 years.

Now let's look at a 15-year mortgage at 3.25 percent on a $200,000 loan (no taxes and insurance).

Mortgage Repayment Summary	
Loan amount	$200,000
Interest rate	3.25%
Mortgage term	15 years
Monthly payment	$1,405.34
Total of 180 payments	$252,960.76
Total interest paid	$52,960.76
Payoff date	July 2029

As I said before in the CD example, the shorter the period of time that money is borrowed for, the less the rate of interest charged to borrow. So just for having full access to the equity in your home 15 years sooner, you will get a 0.75 percent lower interest rate. But how much less will you pay in interest? Try $90,778.25. That's 63 percent less interest than the 30-year fixed-rate mortgage. However, your payment will be 47 percent higher on a monthly basis.

In my estimation, it comes down to one thing. You guessed it: your budget. If you can afford to be smart, then be smart (15-year mortgage). If you can't afford to be smart, then don't be stupid. Trying to get a 15-year mortgage when the payment would hurt you financially on a monthly basis is one of the most foolish things you can do. You need to be realistic. If you can't afford it, you can't afford it. You don't need liquidity if your cash flow is tight; you need "stretched out" payments.

In a perfect world, when you choose to buy a home, get a 15-year mortgage. Doing this will require you buy less house than you could if you took out a 30-year mortgage, but owning your home outright in just 15 years will give you a leg up on your financial life. You haven't even been alive for 30 years. How can you reasonably commit that period of time toward something you can vanquish in 15 years?

Once you hit your forties, a 30-year mortgage begins to commit your retirement income to a mortgage payment. Honestly, can you actually imagine being retired at this point? Probably not. It's likely more than two decades away. There will be five to six more Olympics by the time you retire!

THE IMPORTANCE OF A GOOD REALTOR

I firmly believe in the importance of hiring a competent financial professional to help guide your financial life. This probably doesn't surprise you. What may surprise you is who I think is the most important financial professional in your life. It's not who you think. Consider the choices. Of course there's a financial planner, an insurance agent, an accountant, and even a lawyer. But I believe the most important financial professional in any of our lives is a realtor. A bad realtor can create havoc in your life for 30 years or more, while a great realtor can ensure stress-free living within your financial limits.

Realtors help people make the largest purchase they will ever make and take on more debt than they will ever take on. I don't know about you, but to me, those two factors alone make the realtor the most important financial advisor a person can have.

Here's why most people don't feel like I do: I believe a financial advisor's job—whether the advisor is a stockbroker or a realtor—is to help prevent mistakes. There's an old adage in the investment world: The first step in making money is not losing money. A great financial professional will assess the situation, calculate risks, and advise you on what *not* to do. Show me a financial professional that is a "yes man," and I'll show you a worthless financial advisor.

A great realtor will tell you the truth even when you don't want to hear it. Here are the truths that a great realtor will help you hear.

▶ **Some properties don't appreciate in value and may actually decrease in value, even during normal market conditions.** This is a tough pill to swallow for a new homebuyer—an excited new homebuyer at that. Some brand-new homes fall in value during normal market conditions. This can create a series of very scary problems. Stagnant or falling home values can be especially troubling for people who force themselves into a low-price home in lieu of being a renter.

▶ **Loan approval is not confirmation that a purchase is objectively affordable.** Determining the affordability of a home has become a tremendously subjective process, as you've just learned. A great financial advisor (a realtor) can prevent loan approval from becoming the catalyst of a financial disaster. But what realtor is going to speak up and potentially speak out of place? A good one. A really good one.

▶ **There is a bad time to buy a home.** This has nothing to do with real estate as an investment. In fact, unless you're willing to sell your home at the drop of a hat, then it's not an investment. Calling something an investment often justifies poor decisions. If there's a right time and place to buy a home, then there's obviously a wrong time and place to buy a home. I want a realtor who sings this song.

Find a great realtor. Without a doubt, the biggest financial issues I've seen in people's financial lives over the last 15 years could have been prevented by a difficult conversation with an honest realtor. When a true professional tells you something you don't want to hear, listen harder. Don't dismiss the truth.

HOME IMPROVEMENTS

You wouldn't be alone if you wanted to make major changes to the house you currently live in. If this is the case, you need a strategy to pay for all of these changes. Whether it's a kitchen remodel, a room addition, or even new carpet, deciding how you are going to fund your project can mean the difference between financial bliss and financially frustration.

Without a doubt, one of the most popular ways to fund a home improvement project is with a home equity line of credit (HELOC). As you learned in Chapter 2, a HELOC draws against the equity of your home. Your home *secures* the loan, which technically makes it a secured loan.

There are some advantages to HELOCs. The interest you pay on the loan is deductible on your taxes. The payments can be relatively low and are often spread out over a 10-year period. And most people love the seemingly instant access to this big pile of cash. The problem is that it isn't exactly cash; it's borrowed money. It's stone-cold, raw debt. I'd rather you not tap into your home equity to buy things.

It's only fair that I present a reasonable alternative to home equity loans. In fact, I'm going to suggest something that I personally did for a major home improvement project, which we completed just a few years ago: Save the money for the project. Saving money for a major financial goal is substantially more productive than funding a financial goal with borrowed money. It's the difference between a store credit card and layaway.

Layaway has gotten a weird reputation over the last couple of decades, but why? Layaway employs delayed gratification, while putting a purchase on a credit card employs instant gratification. Which is better? Frankly, delayed gratification is better because instant gratification funded by debt is dangerous. Trust me when I tell you this: I wanted to complete my home improvement project two years before we actually completed it. But we were unwilling to convince ourselves that having it now was more important than exercising financial sensibility.

We should probably look at some numbers. If you were to take out a $15,000 home equity line of credit with a 4.8 percent interest rate, then 10 years' worth of $163/month payments would pay off your debt and cost you $3,742.50 in interest. In this example, you would pay 24.95 percent more for a home improvement project because you didn't have the patience to save money. On the flip side, if you made every effort to pre-fund the home improvement project prior to starting it, you'd eliminate $3,742.50 in interest expenses, develop invaluable saving skills, and avoid 10 years of payments.

Anecdotally, I've found that people tend to exhale after they borrow money. This results in a complete lack of urgency to pay off the debt. They already received the gratification from the purchase, and the "paying for it" portion of the program isn't a lot of fun. However, it won't take anywhere near 10 years to save $15,000. If the rule is that you can't start the project until you save the money, then you will save the money aggressively, efficiently, and quickly.

The next time you think about borrowing money to make a major consumer purchase, consider trusting yourself and the math instead of trusting a payment schedule.

WHAT REALLY ADDS VALUE TO YOUR HOME

The term *home improvement* itself is a sales pitch. Something that is improved must be worth more money, right? I don't know. The operative term that we are dealing with today is *value*. There's personal value and there's resale value. The confusion between the two concepts goes a long way in explaining why people make so many home improvement mistakes.When you are making a home improvement decision, it's important to ask yourself whether more expenses will equal more increased value. There has to be a tipping point, right? There has to be a baseline of some sort. Putting $10,000 into a basement remodel may increase the home's resale value by $10,000, but a $25,000 remodel may only increase the home's resale value by $14,000.

Unfortunately, every situation is different. But you have to have a baseline. You must. Therefore, here is a list, provided by HGTV, of home improvement projects and how much of the expense of the improvement may be recouped by an increase in resale value.

▶ Basement or other unfinished space finishing: 50 to 90 percent. Thus, a $30,000 basement improvement would potentially lead to an increased resale value of $15,000 to $27,000.

▶ Kitchen remodeling: 70 to 120 percent.

▶ Painting: Up to 300 percent.

▶ Bathroom addition: 90 to 130 percent.

▶ Bathroom remodel: 65 to 120 percent.

▶ Window/door replacement: 50 to 90 percent.

▶ Deck addition: 65 to 90 percent.

Almost everyone has heard that swimming pool additions add absolutely no resale value and in some cases can decrease property value based on the high cost of maintenance. But did you know that landscaping doesn't add much value either? It may add curb appeal, but it won't add a great deal of resale value. Both of these things add a great deal of personal value, and if you have the financial resources to fund these purchases, then have at it. But don't assume you'll necessarily see an increase in your property value because of it.

No matter which project you choose, using debt to fund it is not a great idea. Check that: It's a great idea—according to your bank. But then again, tanning is a good idea—according to tanning places. Your house is not a piggy bank! Although you can borrow against it for things that you deem important, you should not do so.

Did I mention that my assertion is now supported by the Great Recession of 2008? The financial meltdown that we are now (arguably) exiting was fueled by homeowners who stripped equity out of their homes. Home improvement projects funded with HELOCs were a bank marketing gimmick gone awry. It was a bad idea then, it's a bad idea now, and it will always be a bad idea. Fund home improvement projects with money you have saved. And by saved, I mean in addition to your emergency fund money (three months of expenses).

But what about sweat equity? Sweat equity is real. Basically, sweat equity is the concept of doing the work yourself and not paying labor costs to finish a home improvement project. If you have the skills, then doing some of the work yourself could really improve your chances of increasing the value of your home in proportion to your expenses. Labor expenses often double the cost of home improvement projects. If you know what you're doing, a $10,000 (with labor) bathroom remodel may cost you only $5,000 if you do the work yourself. This almost guarantees that you will recoup your costs via increased resale value.

However, we now have a potential problem: If you don't have the skills to complete a home improvement project, your attempt to do so could result in big, big trouble. Not only could you ruin something, but you also could break the law, get hurt, and anger your spouse.

The bottom line is pretty simple:

▶ Choose your projects wisely.

▶ Be realistic about how much your home's resale value will actually increase.

▶ Don't go into debt to remodel.

▶ Utilize sweat equity when applicable.

CAR

Among all of the tricky spending categories, you'll find transportation costs. Car payments, car insurance, and gas seem financially innocuous; in reality, they're anything but. There are more ways to mess up your financial life with poor transportation-cost decisions than with decisions in almost any other spending category. You can buy the wrong car, pay too much for it, finance it the wrong way, and then pick the wrong company to insure it. All the while, you are trying to keep your final monthly expenditure under the prescribed 15 percent of your monthly take-home pay. A poor car-buying (or leasing) decision can leave you in the lurch for years.

Consider the story of Ben and Carrie. Ben and Carrie were suburbanites who had been married for about four years and lived in a house they could barely afford from a mortgage-payment standpoint. Whereas I prefer that people keep their monthly mortgage payment around 25 percent of their take-home pay, their payment hovered around 34 percent. Not surprisingly, they were stressed. And despite their mortgage payment being a third higher than it should be, their transportation budget was what really had them in trouble. Ben and Carrie were spending 23 percent of their income on getting to and from work.

Staying under budget can be challenging, especially if you have two car payments, as was the case with Ben and Carrie. To compound their issues, Ben had owed more money on his previous car than it was worth, and he decided to trade it in anyway. Therefore, he did something very common yet very dangerous: He financed negative equity. In other words, he rolled his old loan into his new car loan and essentially paid $34,000 for a $28,000 car. Anecdotally, I've noticed that once people start down this borrowing-decision path, they stay on this path for at least two cars. While a car dealer may present this process as a solution to a transportation problem, it certainly does create a whole other set of problems. So a solution it is not.

In a perfect world, you'd have no car payments. I've personally enjoyed this phenomenon for years now, and I can tell you that there's nothing better. Yet as crazy as this sounds, always having a car payment might be the solution to a transportation budget issue.

Going over your 15 percent transportation budget can create a major cash-flow crunch that hinders your ability to make financial progress in the other areas of your life. And while it may seem as though it always makes sense to temporarily bite the bullet on a higher monthly payment via a car purchase versus a car lease agreement, often it does not. If you are struggling with other forms of debt, are paying too much for housing, and/or are paying out the ear for daycare, then finding a very inexpensive lease might be the best financial decision. Yes, despite what you've heard, a car lease might actually save the financial day.

A car lease can make sense if you're in a cash-flow crunch. However, it is neither a long-term solution nor a blank check to get whatever type of car you want. Preferably, if you're in a cash-flow crunch, you'll just buy a very cheap car for cash, but sometimes that isn't an option. And while I realize that leasing a car isn't technically *great* personal finance advice, it is very *practical* personal finance advice. And the reality is that if you're in a big cash-flow crunch, then you haven't shown the greatest ability to handle technical personal finance decisions, so some practical real-world advice is warranted.

If you choose to lease, make sure you aggressively clean up your financial life during the term of the lease. If it's a three-year lease, then you've got three years to clean up debt, tighten down spending issues, and build cash reserves. The goal in all of this is to make sure you're not spending more than 15 percent of your income on transportation costs (car payments, fuel, and insurance). Feel free to ignore this advice, but don't come to me when you're upset.

BUT REALLY, SHOULD YOU BUY OR LEASE A NEW CAR?

Buying anything new is exciting, but you would be hard pressed to find many things more exciting than buying a new car. Ahh, that new-car smell, that sparkling finish, that crafty finance manager… Huh? You didn't know that the finance director of a car dealership is all part of the experience? Well, then, we have a lot to cover.

Buying a car is not like buying a sandwich. (This observation alone is worth the price of this book.) If you happen to be walking by a deli and you get a hunger pang, you'll likely saunter into said shop and buy a sandwich. Your limitations are quite simple: You either have the money to buy the sandwich or you don't. There's no built-in system that helps your sandwich dreams come true. And if there happened to be a guy who sat in a dark office with the sole purpose of making you a sandwich-owner today with a smile and a handshake, you would probably run. (And, yes, I realize you technically could put the sandwich on your credit card, but just pretend that's not the case, so I can keep this example here. I happen to love the image of a weird sandwich-finance guy sitting in a dark room.) Ahem, back to the car…

So what's different about buying a car? Typically, the missing factor in buying a car is your own affordability awareness. When you buy a sandwich, you know whether or not you can afford it. When buying a car, many people genuinely have no clue. And that is only the first mistake. You need to make many decisions before you ever set foot on the lot. These decisions include how much car you can afford (how much the monthly payment will be), how much your down payment will be, and finally, whether you should buy or lease. This last decision will certainly affect your entire budget.

The option to lease a car has met some bad publicity in the financial world: Many experts feel that leasing is inefficient. Generally speaking, I tend to agree. But leasing a car can be a brilliant way to avoid endless payments for a car you don't want to keep for the long term, or to fit a payment into a tight budget. Let's figure out whether you're one of these types of people.

The first decision you need to make is whether to buy or lease. Look at the following descriptions of a typical car lessee and a typical car buyer and decide which one best describes you.

Typical car lessee

▶ Drives relatively few miles (fewer than 15,000 per year).

▶ Consistently wants a new and/or different type of car every few years. (Is this your vice?)

▶ Needs an affordable (low-payment) short-term solution.

▶ Insists on always having the car covered under warranty.

▶ Takes very good care of the vehicle.

Typical car buyer

▶ Drives an average to high amount (15,000 miles or more per year).

▶ Wants to eventually have no car payment.

▶ Has a greater level of patience with an older car.

▶ Doesn't feel the need to always drive a new car.

▶ Prefers to customize the car.

Which category best describes you?

An oversimplified way to approach this is to decide whether you are someone who insists on always driving a new car. If so, you should consider leasing. Frankly, I don't think that anyone needs to always drive a new car, but I'm not going to waste my time trying to convince you that driving a new car doesn't make sense. If your car is your vice, that's your decision.

Leasing is definitely a worthwhile option for some—but before you commit to it, you should ask yourself the kinds of tough questions you now know to ask before making financial decisions. Do you really need to lease? Could the funds be better spent or saved? Is there room in your budget for a lease? If the answer to many of these questions is no and if you are the average person who just needs a reliable set of wheels to go to and fro, you should be buying, not leasing, a car.

YOUR NEXT CAR PURCHASE

Even if you have determined that your car is your vice and that you want to buy rather than lease, this doesn't mean you should go wild; you will still need to make an intelligent decision. Whether you decide to buy with a loan or take a lease-to-buy option, the goal should be to pay for the car as quickly as possible. Stretching out a car loan or committing to a longer lease is a bad idea. Longer contracts mean less flexibility, and less flexibility means that other financial goals don't get the attention they deserve. You might be tempted to spread out your financing to lower your monthly payment, but the real solution is to buy a less expensive car.

The ideal situation is to bypass a car payment altogether by pre-funding the purchase. This might mean buying a used car or a less expensive one, both of which are far better options than the alternatives: getting locked into high monthly payments or buying a car you can't afford. But I do realize that pre-funding isn't always possible. Here's how to make a car-buying decision that won't destroy your entire budget.

To start, don't finance a car for longer than five years (three is ideal). It would be nice to buy a brand-new car, but when you try to fit your transportation costs into your budget, you will probably have to make cuts somewhere. So, consider buying a certified pre-owned car—a relatively new car that is still under warranty from the manufacturer. Buying a certified pre-owned car strikes the right balance of frugality and practicality. Don't focus solely on the affordability of your car payment. (This holds true whether you buy or lease.) Consider all of the costs involved in transportation (gas, maintenance, and insurance).

You should keep your total transportation costs under 15 percent of your net household income, regardless of whether your household needs one or two cars. If your net monthly income is $4,000, your total transportation costs should be no more than $600.

These may seem like severe restrictions, but if you want to spend more on transportation than prescribed, you will need to make the proper changes to your budget. In other words, feel free to spend more, but know you will need to make significant cutbacks in your budget to allow for this.

Let's see how transportation costs affect your current or future driving situation.

What is your net monthly household income?	$
What is 15 percent of your net monthly household income?	$

How do your current transportation costs compare to this number? Let's take a look, starting with monthly costs.

Current car payment	$
Current monthly fuel cost	$
Current monthly insurance cost	$
Total monthly costs	$

Now, your current annual costs.

Maintenance	$
Oil-change costs	$
Tires	$
Car washes	$
Repairs	$
Total maintenance	$
Monthly maintenance (the total above, divided by 12)	$

Do you have to keep your transportation costs below 15 percent to be a financial success? No. But you must be willing to adjust your spending in other areas.

COLLEGE EDUCATION

Do you believe your child's education to be a purchase or an investment? It's a pretty wild debate, if you ask me. I'd argue that your end of the bargain is a purchase, and anything your child pays for is an investment. Your child will have a return on his or her investment, and you will gain satisfaction from your purchase.

But whether you like it or not, in the eyes of the federal government, you are at least partially responsible for paying for your adult child's (18 to 23 years old) education. This has long been the case. The Department of Education, college and universities, and the rest of the federal government also need you to know that if students want to borrow money on their own to fund their education, without the help of their parents, the parents will still likely be required to fund a portion of the education.

As you learned in Chapter 2, the FAFSA (Free Application For Student Aid) often dictates how much money you and your children will pay for their education. If your children are to get any aid at all, they must use your financial information on the FAFSA.

In case you're wondering, children can exclude their parents' financial information on the FAFSA, which increases the students' chances for receiving more financial aid, only *if* they are emancipated from their parents. What makes an adult child emancipated from the parent? A few things do, among them having a child of their own, being married, or joining the military. Other than that, if an adult is 23 years old or younger, his or her parents' financial information will determine how much college will cost. Students can't ask for student loans without providing their parent's financial information.

Saving for college has become increasingly difficult for American families. There are two primary reasons for this: (1) decreasing financial sensibility, and (2) college price inflation.

College education has become increasingly inefficient. Whereas technology is leveraged in many industries to decrease consumer costs, colleges (for the most part) have refused to pass on the savings to consumers. How does it still take 48 months of a person's life to get a college education? Some colleges and universities are catching on and allowing students to earn a four-year degree in just three years. This is mainly accomplished with online courses. But for the most part, when you go to college, you're looking at four years of schooling, minimum. Not only that, but colleges have been able to take advantage of student loan subsidization and push college costs even higher. Check out this chart from FinAid.org. It shows college inflation compared to general inflation. College inflation is almost double general inflation. That's not cool.

Year	College Inflation	General Inflation	Rate Ratio
1958–1996	7.24%	4.49%	1.61
1977–1986	9.85%	6.72%	1.47
1987–1996	6.68%	3.67%	1.82
1958–2001	6.98%	4.30%	1.62
1979–2001	7.37%	3.96%	1.86
1992–2001	4.77%	2.37%	2.01
1985–2001	6.39%	3.18%	2.01
1958–2005	6.89%	4.15%	1.66
1989–2005	5.94%	2.99%	1.99

Since the U.S. government is guaranteeing student loans, more students can borrow. Which in turn means that demand for a college education is high. And competition to attract and retain students is even higher. This leads to some pretty nutty stuff. Why does your college have a climbing wall? Why does your alma mater have dorms nicer than most three-star hotels? All of these amenities cost money, and you are paying for it. Well, student loans are paying for it.

Am I against sending your child to college? Absolutely not. However, I *am* against cost inefficiency. I encourage you to seek out institutions that honor their commitment to their students' financial futures. For instance, some colleges have begun to offer four-year degrees that students can earn in just three years. This reduces student tuition costs by 25 percent. That makes sense to me. Does it make sense to you?

The easiest way to pay for college is to fund this goal over time. If you start saving right away, then time becomes your friend. If you wait until your kid is old enough to spell "college," then time is your enemy. Here's what I mean:

- ▶ $200 saved per month for 18 years (started the month your child is born) at a hypothetical 8 percent rate of return will give you $97,071.03 by the time college rolls around.

- ▶ $200 saved per month for 12 years (started on your child's sixth birthday) at a hypothetical 8 percent rate of return will give you $49,188.71 by the time college rolls around.

Waiting just six years cuts your college savings *in half!* That's not good, but it's math. So don't fight math—use it.

College financial aid is one of the most misunderstood concepts in finance, from the snout down to the tail. We first must examine why financial aid is given and in what form. One of the most frustrating aspects of this conversation for parents is that the United States Department of Education (DoE) has a much different definition of need than parents do, and the DoE's idea is the only idea that matters.

Financial aid means many things. It means student loans, both public and private. It means scholarships. It means grants. And it means a bunch of other random stuff. When you seek aid, you simply are looking ways to pay for school, ideally in ways that lessen the cost. When the DoE gets involved—and they almost always do—two things are determined: how much you are expected to personally pay and how much you will easily be able to borrow. That leaves out one weird factor: how much you *need* to borrow.

We should start with what you are responsible for. This is called your *Expected Family Contribution* (EFC), and we discussed it briefly in Chapter 2. I ran some info through an EFC calculator to help illustrate the DoE's perspective. I don't know your particulars, so I ran some random numbers through the calculator. Here are the numbers I used:

▶ Household income: $75,000

▶ Investments: $50,000

▶ Cash, checking, and savings: $5,000

▶ Parents' ages: 45

Based on the estimates above, the fake family I created would be responsible for somewhere between $6,400 and $8,800 per year in college costs. As CollegeData.com notes:

> "Your real cost—also called your net price—includes your EFC, plus any financial need that your college doesn't cover and any financial aid in the form of loans or earnings from work-study. You will have to cover any unmet financial need from your own resources, repay loans, and work the hours required for work-study aid. The real cost of attending a college includes all the dollars you must spend out of your own pocket, either now or later."

All this is to suggest that someone in your house is going to be borrowing a significant amount of money unless your children receive merit-based scholarships or they go to an inexpensive school. You will get some financial aid, but you should be more concerned about covering your EFC. You will most likely fund this with your 529, your current income (when they are in college), and additional borrowing.

Don't wait to start taking your kids' college educations seriously. Reactively funding a college education can send shockwaves through your financial life that can permanently damage your chances for a successful and comfortable retirement.

THE FINAL FACTOR IN MAKING BIG PURCHASES

Perfect. You did the math. You saved the money. And now it's time to make one of the biggest purchases you will ever make. But there's one more thing: You need to qualify for credit. If borrowing money is part of your plan to buy a house or car, then the lending institution will use your credit report as a means to make your dream come true or to turn your dream into a nightmare.

But as you'll learn, when you are declined credit, sometimes it's a good thing.

CHAPTER 6

THE PICTURE: CREDIT

I have a secret. I'm going to share it with you, but you must be willing to ignore everything you've heard about the importance of credit scores. The older you get, the less your credit score actually matters. There, I said it. I know, I'm a heretic, right? I don't tell you this in an effort to appear contrarian. I simply need you to know that you should be getting close to wrapping up your borrowing career.

What does a credit score measure? It measures how good you are at borrowing money. I don't want to be good at borrowing money, because I don't want to borrow money. Sure, you'll need to borrow money to buy your home, but aside from that it's quite possible to live your life without really borrowing money. The challenge is that to borrow money for something like a house, you need to demonstrate your ability to successfully borrow smaller amounts of money. Seems simple, right? Nope. At one point in time, it *was* that simple. Today? Well, it's no longer simple. Credit scores today do more to induce borrowing than they do to discourage borrowing.

If I had to oversimplify a healthy timeline of a person's relationship with debt, it would go like this: Establish credit, buy a house, and then be done with credit. Every day, people all around the world make this choice. Whether you choose to is up to you. But it wouldn't be fair for me to leave our discussion on credit at that. You need to understand how the system works, regardless of whether you choose to be part of it.

When you don't have enough money to buy something outright, you may seek credit to help complete the purchase. An institution's willingness to extend you credit is based on several factors, including your income, your assets, and your credit report. If your level of income, assets, and credit report looks subjectively good to a lender, they will make credit available to you.

It's not uncommon for people to associate this available credit with purchasing power. They rationalize, "If a credit institution is willing to issue me credit, they must have confidence in my ability able to pay it off." But a credit institution has just a little conflict of interest when it comes to determining what you can and cannot afford, wouldn't you say? If you need an example, just think about all those people whose creditors gave them a vote of confidence to buy houses they couldn't afford.

So what's the point of having good credit if you can't afford to use it to buy the things you want?

That's the great financial paradox. You want to obtain and build credit so that you qualify to receive the best terms possible from creditors, in the event that you want to borrow money. (After all, without good credit how are you going to be able to afford those things that you can't pay for completely up front in cash, but that you actually *can* afford, such as a house?) On the flip side, if you *do* qualify for good credit terms, it's likely because you're the type of person who would never think of using credit to buy things you can't realistically afford (or aren't able to pay off within a reasonable amount of time).

In fact, a person can "earn" a great credit score despite being a financial disaster by any acceptable measure.

Consider the following large numbers:

- ▶ $210,000
- ▶ $85,000
- ▶ $165,000

These are the amounts of credit card debt that I saw people have in a two-week period in the spring of 2014. While you are recovering from the shock of seeing numbers that high, allow me to knock you over. In all three cases, the people had amazing credit.

Good credit. Bad credit. Who cares? It's the attitude of borrowing that's the problem, not the interest rates that come and go with good or bad credit. In one instance (from the debt numbers above), the person had a 785 credit score. His *great* credit score allowed him to constantly borrow and put himself $85,000 into debt. Along with his behavior and decision-making, his credit score ruined his financial life. Credit scores *are not* a measure of financial health. I repeat for the 10 millionth time, your credit score, good or bad, doesn't tell your financial story. It simply tells your borrowing story. You want to know the real story? Look at a person's net worth. And here's some good news: We'll do that in the next chapter. But now back to your borrowing story.

The point of getting and improving your credit is not so that you can buy more things. Good credit is important because:

▶ **Healthy credit indicates healthy habits.** As far as many decision makers are concerned, discipline and structure in one aspect of your life tend to be good indications of a consistent pattern of responsible habits. Your credit is one of the easiest entry points of assessment, which is why you need to determine your credit health today.

▶ **Some employers are now running credit checks.** Can you imagine being the best candidate for a job but losing out on it because you have bad credit? Federal law prevents employers from discriminating based on bankruptcy, but employers are allowed to base their hiring decisions on collection actions and defaults.

▶ **You need at least decent credit to set up basic household utilities, such as electricity, water, and phone service.** A seemingly harmless series of impulsive credit card purchases that wind up doing near-fatal damage to your credit score can create a nightmare when you try to set up accounts with utility companies. What's it going to be? Stuff? Or electricity, gas, and running water? (This is not a trick question. The answer is electricity, gas, and running water.)

▶ **In many instances, poor credit will prevent you from renting an apartment or house.** Being denied a mortgage is one thing; being denied a place to rent, though? That puts you in a completely different category. It means you'll be stuck at home with mom and dad. You can imagine what this type of situation does for relationships and boundaries.

▶ **Many property and casualty (auto, renters', and homeowners') insurance companies will charge you a higher monthly premium if you have suspect credit.** Yep, it's the equivalent of a health insurance company charging higher premiums for those with high cholesterol, high blood pressure, and obesity. The company essentially sees a higher risk and sets fees accordingly.

HOW DO I FIND OUT WHERE I STAND WITH CREDITORS?

There's a simple answer to this question: Order a credit report. If you have good credit, your credit report will simply reinforce the importance of your good financial habits. If you have bad credit, your credit report will confirm your need to develop new financial habits and get rid of old ones. If you have no idea what to expect either way, there's even more incentive for you to order a copy today.

You can order your credit report online at www.Annual-CreditReport.com. You might be wondering why I chose AnnualCreditReport.com over the other credit-reporting services out there. You might also be wondering why some services are free while others charge you fees.

The basic credit report obtained from AnnualCreditReport. com won't give you your credit score, but it *will* give you your credit history. I find that people who manage their credit health by aiming to reach an arbitrarily selected credit score aren't as successful as those who manage their credit by continually improving their financial habits.

WHAT TO LOOK FOR ON YOUR CREDIT REPORT

Now that you have your credit report, what are you supposed to do with it? For now, you want to familiarize yourself with the rich information it provides you. Look at the following items to see where you stand:

▶ **Total Accounts.** This is the total number of accounts listed on your credit history. As with most items on your credit report, this number can vary with each credit-reporting agency.

▶ **Open Accounts.** This is the total number of accounts you currently have open—regardless of whether they have balances. A zero-balance account is still considered open.

▶ **Closed Accounts.** This lists all closed credit lines. This could include old mortgages, closed credit cards, or paid-off student loans.

▶ **Delinquent.** This section details any accounts for which you are behind on payments. Inevitably, this is the section that surprises most people. It is not uncommon to find delinquent accounts that you didn't know about.

▶ **Derogatory.** Whereas a 30-day late payment is considered delinquent, a 60-day late payment is considered derogatory. This section is the most important, as anything really hurting your credit will show up here.

▸ **Balances.** What do you owe the world? More specifically, what do you owe your creditors? That number will show up in this section, and it can be pretty scary if you've taken out expensive loans for things such as a mortgage or college tuition.

▸ **Payments.** This section lists your monthly debt obligations. This will include your monthly mortgage and/or car payments, and minimum payments on your credit card(s) and other loans.

▸ **Public Records.** This section lets you know if your credit problems have become public record. It includes liens, foreclosures, bankruptcies, and legal judgments. This section will also list any changes in your marital status and whether you have sought professional credit counseling.

▸ **Inquiries (Two Years).** This section indicates which people or institutions have requested your credit report in the last two years. These inquiries are usually the result of your requests or applications to borrow money from an institution. This is called a *hard inquiry*. A hard inquiry is one initiated by someone on the verge of lending you money per your request, whereas a *soft inquiry* is initiated by someone checking your credit to see whether you are a good credit risk. A soft inquiry is usually performed by an insurance company or an employer. Too many hard inquiries are a bad thing and will harm your credit.

Full disclosure: I went seven years without checking my credit report. It wasn't because I didn't think it was important, it was because I didn't think I had a reason to check it. I paid my bills on time, I didn't miss payments, and I made enough money to cover my purchases. When I finally took the time to check my credit, however, I was shocked to find that I had an account in collection. Considering my spending habits, I was furious that my credit report didn't reflect my stellar (if I do say so myself) spending habits, but the explanation for my problem was quite simple: I never closed an old checking account. In my mind, I was done using it, but instead of closing it I let it sit unused for four years. There was $50 in the account when I stopped using it, and over the years I started acquiring inactivity fees—$3 per month, to be exact. The account fell below zero, and the bank was unable to contact me at my old business address. That's when the account went into collection, sending "Perfect Credit Pete" to the dark side. I was able to make the proper arrangements to pay the fee and get my credit headed back in the right direction. The lesson? Register for a free credit report every year, and take the time to review it and follow up on any negative findings. Otherwise, you could be in for some nasty credit surprises in the future.

REPAIR AND BUILD YOUR CREDIT

As you may have gathered, I'm a big advocate for improving spending habits rather than focusing on credit scores. But because improving your habits will improve your credit score and because this number will play an important role once your financial life is back in order, it's important that you understand how these two things are related.

As you decide whether your credit is truly in need of repair, be mindful of the lessons Lassie taught us. When I was a kid, I would watch reruns of *Lassie*. I knew they were reruns because they were in black and white, and the characters said words like "golly" and "shucks." The premise of the show was pretty simple: A kid would fall in a well, and his paramedic collie would get help. The kid's name was Timmy. He couldn't stay out of the darn well. Every day he would eat his country breakfast, then he'd go fall in a well. He, his parents, and his community were the least self-aware people on the planet. Well, except for Lassie. Lassie was a dog. Timmy was a resilient little person. He'd fall in the well, get rescued, learn nothing from it, and then end up back in the well by 10:00 the next morning. In other words, Timmy was setting himself up to deal with credit repair in the twenty-first century.

America is Timmy. We frequently trap ourselves in wells, get rescued, and then run back to the well. All the while, we celebrate our multiple renaissances, while learning nothing from them in the process. Your goal isn't to fix your credit so that you can buy more stuff at lower interest rates, although that's how marketers, including credit counseling marketers, market to us.

Again, fixing your credit so that you can borrow money isn't what you are supposed to do. Right now you're thinking, "Yes, it is." No, it's not. If you climb out of the well of poor credit for the sole purpose of going back into the well, you are a Timmy.

Don't repair your credit so that you can go back to the bottom of the well. Repair your credit so that you can move on with your life. Repair your credit so you can close that chapter in your life permanently. You don't have to play the borrow-money game. Assets can buy things just as credit can buy things.

But before you can put credit and debt in your past, you must first fully understand how it works.

WHAT YOUR CREDIT SCORE MEANS

Assigning a numeric value to your credit profile is a structured way for creditors (as well as employers and utility and insurance companies) to gauge your credit standing relative to others.

Your credit score will range somewhere between 300 and 850. As a point of reference, a score of 700 puts you in a better position than 61 percent of the nation. And a score of 765 puts you ahead of 84 percent of your fellow Americans. One of the most common questions people ask me is, "What qualifies as a good credit score?" While I often hesitate to answer the question (because I find it to be irrelevant), the answer is 725. A score of 725 is technically good. But anything above 700 should allow you to receive the credit lending terms that you desire.

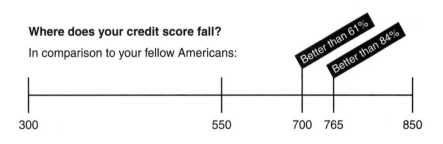

Where does your credit score fall?

In comparison to your fellow Americans:

Better than 61%

Better than 84%

300   550   700   765   850

Don't get me wrong: Having a point of reference against which to gauge your relative standing is definitely a positive thing, but as humans we always manage to make things more confusing than they need be. Take, for example, my personal credit score. It has a 69-point spread, which means that among the three major credit-reporting agencies, one of them rates me 69 points higher than the lowest agency's scoring model. What am I to gather from this? That's easy: I shouldn't manage the score; I should manage my habits. If you manage your habits, your credit score will take care of itself, and eventually you can use it as a tool to track your progress.

IS IT REALLY FIXED?

Does your credit look broken? Do you need to head down the arduous path of fixing your credit? "Broken" is my highly technical term for a credit report that contains any negative elements that affect your credit. Your credit as a whole may or may not be broken, but we want to address anything that needs improvement. Of course, when it comes to fixing broken credit, there's a catch: You can't technically fix it.

Why not? Well, your past indiscretions can't be fully erased. Your financial history will always be a part of your credit record. The good news is that you can significantly improve your credit, and with a little time and effort it will get better.

WHAT CREDIT SCORES AND DIETING HAVE IN COMMON

Many people assess their credit health based on their ability to meet a credit score that falls into some lender's definition of "good credit." My suggestion is to think about your credit score as weight on a scale. The number you see there is not in and of itself a measure of whether you're overweight or too thin—to determine that, you would need to know other details, such as height, muscle mass, and the like—but it does have value as an indication of your relative progress (or setback) over time.

Think about it: Many variables factor into a person's weight, so when creating dieting benchmarks, you have to take into consideration factors such as bone structure, age, muscular composition, and so on, rather than trying to meet a goal set forth by a universal weight chart that maps out pounds versus height. Everyone will have different diet goals based on his or her own unique combination of contributing variables.

So, just as you wouldn't base your diet success on meeting a weight that doesn't take into consideration your body type, you shouldn't base your credit health on a score that doesn't factor in your starting point, the steps you're taking to improve it, and the healthy spending habits you're developing as a result. That's a surefire recipe for disappointment. Instead, you should view a rise or fall in your credit score as a means of calibrating your habits to offset setbacks or perpetuate progress.

So how do you get started?

THREE STEPS TO IMPROVING BAD CREDIT (OR TO MAINTAINING GOOD CREDIT)

While I don't believe you should focus on having a great credit score for the sake of having a great credit score, I do believe you should improve bad credit habits and maintain the healthy credit habits you already possess. The following steps will allow you to right the wrongs and put your credit worries behind you permanently.

1. **Look for any disputable items on your credit report.** Because I'm an eternal optimist, I tend to think that if there's a blemish on my credit report, it can't possibly be my fault. Of course, this might be more delusional than optimistic, but you should start your credit-repair process by going through your credit report closely to make sure that there are no inaccuracies, such as a misspelled name, credit lines that you never applied for, or obvious cases of identity theft.

2. **Dispute any inaccuracies.** There are several ways to dispute inaccuracies on your credit report that don't require working with a credit-repair service. These services don't do anything you can't do on your own. But if you don't want to go through the process of disputing these items, you can certainly hire a professional to help.

   Assuming you decide to go it alone, begin by filling out the online form at one of the credit bureau's websites or by calling their toll-free phone number.

▶ Experian (Experian.com): 1-888-397-3742

▶ TransUnion (Transunion.com): 1-800-916-8800

▶ Equifax (Equifax.com): 1-800-685-1111

As you go through your credit report, keep in mind that many of the items you might think are disputable actually aren't. For instance, people often want to dispute the timing of a payment but lack the documentation to support the dispute. There isn't a single person with bad credit who doesn't believe he or she paid a bill within the given grace period. Can you imagine if credit agencies addressed this type of dispute?

The following table will give you a good idea of what you should contest and what you shouldn't even bother with.

Disputable	Nondisputable*
Timing of payments (with documentation)	Timing of payments (without documentation)
Fraud	Level of interest you are being charged
Outdated information	Your own poor decision-making
Clerical errors, such as incorrect name, address, or account number	Whether bankruptcy is your fault

*If what you've identified as an inaccuracy is not disputable, you'll have to improve your credit report the old-fashioned way. See Step 3 to learn how.

3. **Pay your bills on time.** A person with a modest credit
   score can improve his or her score as much as 20 points
   by simply paying bills on time for one month. If this is
   an area where you could stand to improve, make it
   your goal to make at least the minimum payment on
   each of your bills this month. Then try to do the same
   each month after that.

HOW YOUR SCORE IS CALCULATED

As you know, I'm not big on obsessing over your credit score.
My theory is that if you have good, sensible financial habits,
then your score will follow. Plenty of people out there will
show you how to manipulate your credit score to make it go up,
but what's the point? Who are you really tricking? If you have
a high score but a terrible financial situation, then you lose.
You'll just trick someone into loaning you money despite the
fact that you shouldn't be loaned money. This is bad for you,
not them.

The purpose of a credit score is to measure your risk of default.
Although the exact formula for calculating a credit score isn't
known, we do know there are various factors with varying
degrees of importance. In this section, you will see how FICO
(Fair, Isaac, and Company) begins to determine your score.

▶ **Payment history (35 percent).** Are you making payments on time? I hope so. There isn't anything more
   basic than paying your bills on time. Pay your bills on
   time, and your score will remain in a decent place. Pay

your bills 30 days late or more, and your score will suffer, as it should. The entire point of credit is to allow someone to take possession of a good or service now and to pay for it at a later date. If you pay late, you destroy this paradigm.

▶ **Amounts owed (30 percent).** If your credit limit is $5,000 and your balance is $3,500, then your score is going to take a hit. This concept is called *credit utilization*. If you have too much of your total credit in use, your score will go down. If your credit line increases, then your credit might actually improve. For instance, let's say you have $3,000 limit with a $1,700 balance. If your limit were to increase to $10,000, then your credit score would go up because you have a better utilization ratio. This fact is one of the primary reasons why I think credit scores can lead a person astray.

▶ **Credit history (15 percent).** Did you file bankruptcy? Did you have an account in collections? You can try to justify these things however you like, but you aren't the ideal credit risk if you have a spotty credit history. People often wonder whether they should close a credit card they're not using. Closing a card is likely to hurt your credit score, but that doesn't mean you shouldn't do it. If your credit is solid and you don't have a need for the account (you don't), then close it. Having a bunch of store credit cards open will do more harm than good in the long run.

▶ **Inquiries, new credit (10 percent).** When your credit is run several times in an attempt to borrow money, your credit score can take a hit. The more inquiries there are on your credit, the more your score goes down.

Don't ever have anyone run your score unless you know you are going to buy from them.

▶ **Types of credit in use (10 percent).** To be honest, this one is stupid. My mortgage company recently told me that I should open a store credit card and a major credit card (Visa, MasterCard, and so on) to improve my credit. My credit score is very, very good. In my opinion, the mortgage company is giving dangerous advice. While it would technically improve someone's score to have diverse types of credit, the benefit would be minimal because this factor is only 10 percent of the score.

So there it is, good or bad. Do smart things to improve your credit. Pay your bills on time. Don't wildly seek more credit. Don't let accounts go into collections. You can't get too bent out of shape about a bad credit score, and your default solution to any problem shouldn't be to borrow. Besides, if you make every decision based on your credit score, you'll actually end up with a tremendous amount of debt.

YOUR KIDS' CREDIT

While your relationship with credit and debt may be coming to a sweet end, if you have children who are on the cusp of adulthood, then they are likely to be in the courtship phase of their relationship with credit. It is important that you support them in their efforts to establish credit; however, it's very important that you don't *support* them in their efforts to establish credit.

As you may or may not know, some lending institutions ask for a cosigner when the primary borrower doesn't appear to be a good credit risk. And if your young-adult children have no credit, then they are viewed as high credit risks. Lending institutions generally aren't willing to take on the risks that are associated with someone with no credit history, and that's why they want someone else to take the risk: you. The lender wants you to cosign to assume the risk of the borrower.

When you become a cosigner, you are essentially promising to pay back the loan in the event the primary borrower can't handle the loan payments. At first glance, it doesn't necessarily sound like a terrible idea, but it is. With very few exceptions, I find cosigning to be an irresponsible step to take, for both you and your adult child.

You shouldn't take on a risk that a lending institution isn't willing to take on. And, you shouldn't help your kids circumvent a very important step in the credit process. Your children need to learn how to handle credit and debt. They need to learn these concepts from the ground up. If you jump into the fray with them and remove an important step in the process, then how are you helping them? I frequently see an extension of this same problem when parents gift or loan down-payment money to their adult children to help them purchase their first home. Creating the illusion of financial stability isn't a step toward financial stability, it's a step toward danger.

I believe most people are put in a tough situation when asked to cosign, and they generally acquiesce due to guilt. Don't get me wrong; there's a ton of pressure and emotion revolving around cosigning. "Don't you trust me?" the borrower might ask. But cosigning isn't about trust, it's about risk. Risk and trust have very little to do with each other. Do you know who specializes in risk assessment? Lending institutions. Do you know who doesn't specialize in risk assessment? Biased family members. As much scrutiny and criticism as banks receive, they still serve an important purpose with regard to loan underwriting. If a bank says no, then why should you say yes? When you cosign, you are essentially underwriting a sub-prime loan. This is tricky territory. People love to get mad at banks for loaning money to people they shouldn't. Why would you loan money to someone you shouldn't?

This isn't a credit score discussion, either. Earlier this year, a young guy came to me with no credit. In the eyes of the credit agencies, he hadn't done enough to register a blip on their screens. I started poking around this guy's finances and quickly realized that he was doing a remarkable job of making financial decisions. He had very few financial obligations, and he had accumulated $50,000 in savings. He wanted to buy a home. I directed him to a lending institution that I knew would assess the risk involved with lending to someone with no credit. They assessed the risk and decided that his credit score, or lack thereof, was irrelevant. They loaned him money to buy a house.

As clichéd as it has become, isn't this an extension of the participation-trophy problem? There's no way that every kid deserves a trophy, and there's no way everyone has earned the right to borrow money. Not everyone has proven himself or herself to be a good risk. Family members shouldn't mess up this financial natural selection. Your kid isn't missing out when a bank tells him or her no. It's feedback. Your kid is being told he hasn't done enough to display his credit worthiness. Credit rejection isn't a bad thing. When someone is denied a loan, it should be celebrated. Unfortunately, most people view a loan declination as some sort of insult. It's not. You *should* take no for an answer. Take that no, work on your skills, and then come back later to get a yes. How long will your child need to wait? Longer than he or she wants to. But that's okay.

It's not that different from letting your kid ride a carnival ride, despite the fact he isn't quite tall enough. Sure, you can probably talk your way past the carnie, but *should* you?

WHAT IF YOUR KIDS HAVE NO CREDIT AT ALL?

Credit cards are unnecessary once you have an established credit history. And in fact, I believe regular credit card use induces superfluous spending. Points, cash back, and other reward programs wouldn't exist if they didn't increase bank revenue via increased consumerism. This is exactly why I don't use a credit card and why I urge other established individuals to avoid using them. However, I do believe that a credit card is incredibly necessary to establish credit for those individuals who have no credit, especially your young-adult children.

Two groups of people want their credit score to go up: people with damaged credit and people with no credit. We've already discussed improving damaged credit, but now we'll discuss establishing credit when you or your children have none. When you have no credit, life can get incredibly difficult and frustrating. A person with no credit simply hasn't borrowed money that is reflected on his or her credit report. This leads to denials for new credit, increased rental costs, and the need for a cosigner. Which brings us to possibly the most frustrating question in personal finance: How in the world are you supposed to establish credit if people keep denying you because you don't have any established credit?

The answer to this question is so shockingly simple that your head will spin: They need to get a credit card. I know; they've already tried that. But they did it wrong. Before we go much further, I need to draw a line in the sand. While I don't believe people with established credit should use a credit card, I *do* believe people with no credit should use a credit card to establish credit. I realize you might think I'm splitting hairs to make a point, but I assure you I'm not. Think of it this way: You needed training wheels when you first learned to ride your bike, yet you don't use them now. You *could* use them. There are still advantages to using them, but you *don't* use them. This is exactly what you need to do with a credit card. You just need the right type of credit card.

Your kids need a secured credit card. A secured credit card is secured by a cash deposit. Specifically, people send the credit card company a check or money order for $200 to $1,000 to secure the credit line. The credit card company doesn't have to trust that they will pay their credit card bill, because they already have their money. Think of it like a refillable gift card that reports to the credit agencies. When people make a purchase, they create a debt on the card. To establish a credit history, they will make a payment on that debt to bring their security deposit back to its original amount. For instance, if they start with a $200 security deposit, spend $50 on shoes, and then at the end of the month send $50 to the credit card company to take their balance back to the $200 deposited, the bank will report this credit activity to the credit agencies. This establishes credit in a safe way. And did I mention that your kids will get their deposit back when they're finished? No, of course I didn't mention that until now.

The point of this exercise isn't to buy things that they can't afford. The point is to buy things they *can* afford so they can demonstrate their ability to pay back their debts on schedule.

There are some other considerations. They shouldn't leave a balance on the card greater than 50 percent of the entire credit line. For example, if they have $200 deposited, they shouldn't build up debts over $99. If they do, they will have a high credit utilization ratio, and this can affect their credit score negatively. Additionally, they will need/want to continue putting small purchases on this card for about 12 months to establish credit. They can always deposit more cash into the security deposit to increase their credit line, but they shouldn't get too carried away. The point of this exercise is to establish their credit for a few very important reasons, which we'll discuss in a moment. Oh, and they better not miss a payment. They will go from having no credit to having damaged credit, and that's a transition they don't want to make.

When your kids have no credit, their auto insurance, renters insurance, and homeowners insurance costs can be higher than they otherwise would be. If they have no credit, they may have trouble renting a home or an apartment. And if they have no credit, it will be very difficult to get a mortgage, no matter how great the rest of their financial life is. Some financial institutions do something called *manual underwriting*. This is a loan-evaluation process in which a person's non-credit factors are weighed differently from a conventional underwriting process. And while I've seen individuals utilize this process in the past, it's no sure thing.

Establishing credit will let your children do all sorts of other things. However, many of these things aren't so great. Established credit will allow them to get store credit cards, car loans, and unsecured credit cards. I find all three of these uses of credit to be unnecessary. Your kids used training wheels to learn to ride a bike; make sure to tell them to take off the training wheels once they learn to ride.

BEYOND CREDIT

A credit card can render itself pointless once your score is established and you have money. A great credit score and solid credit aren't about enhancing your life; they're about not being inconvenienced by the requirements of those that judge us by our credit history.

It is my sincere belief that your goal should be to rectify your credit and debt past and then be done with it. At one point in your life, the solution may have been to borrow. But you need to put yourself into a position in which borrowing isn't necessary. We're talking self-sufficiency here. Retirement, as a concept, deals with self-sufficiency. As you start to creep toward retirement, you need to eliminate your dependency on not only borrowed money, but also your income itself. You can't cut your dependency on your income if you are dependent on borrowed money.

The more you mess with credit, the less you're focusing on what's really important on your balance sheet: building assets.

CHAPTER 7

THE PIGGY BANK: SAVING AND INVESTING

There is a gigantic difference between saving and investing. You need to know how to do both. Each requires specific skills and rudimentary habits. And while the terms *saving* and *investing* are often used interchangeably, they shouldn't be.

The purpose of saving is threefold. First, saving allows you to handle short-term, unexpected expenses. We sometimes call these types of things *emergencies*, but they aren't always emergencies. Vacations, home furnishings, and car purchases made with cash aren't emergencies, yet they should be funded with savings, not with investments.

The second purpose for savings is to preserve money without taking risks. Although it may seem counterintuitive, you shouldn't be overly concerned with the rate of return you are receiving on your savings account. Saving itself isn't concerned with growth; it's concerned with preservation. Although some investments may be allocated toward preservation-type goals, investments are usually earmarked for appreciation or income-production. But when investing gets involved in the conversation, the word *risk* arrives with it. Savings generally maintains an absence of risk.

The last purpose of saving is also the most important. By saving a portion of your current income now, you are declaring your independence from your total income. The more money you save on a monthly basis, the less likely you are to develop dependence on that portion of your income. If you want to avoid living paycheck to paycheck in the negative sense, your spending must remain independent of your increasing income throughout your career. Otherwise, no matter how much you earn, you'll find a way to spend it.

You need to understand how different types of investments work. You need to know how they are different and which ones are right for you. While a financial advisor would certainly be able to assist you with this, it's in your best interest to have a better than cursory understanding of the investment world.

Regardless of whether you are saving money or investing money, you are increasing your net worth.

THE ROLE OF NET WORTH AS A WEALTH-BUILDING TOOL

Net worth is the greatest metric in all of the financial world. It's a powerful, misunderstood tool that can drive wealth higher, and better yet, pull desperate people out of the doldrums of debt.

Why is net worth such a great measure? Simply put, it measures various financial activities in a very complex way. If you monitor your net worth, you will be able to see the impact of making debt payments, saving money, and investing money, and you can even watch your investments' market performance or simple appreciation. You can obtain your net worth by subtracting your current debts from your current assets. As you know, assets are things such as real estate, savings, and investments. And debts are...debts.

Let's take a look at a couple of different examples to help you better understand this. First up, let's examine the financial life of 48-year-old marketing executive Marcus.

January 1, 2014

Assets:	**$1,012,000**
House:	$389,000
401(k):	$235,000
Company stock:	$78,000
Savings:	$40,000
IRA:	$120,000
Rental property:	$150,000
Debts:	**$150,000**
Mortgage:	$120,000
Rental property mortgage:	$30,000
Net worth:	**$862,000**

As you can clearly see, Marcus' net worth is $862,000. If Marcus continues to take care of business, then he can make some great financial progress. For instance, over the next year, if Marcus pays his mortgage (12 months of principal payments for a total of $9,000 toward his principal), pays his rental property mortgage (12 months of principal payments for a total of $11,000 toward his principal), puts money into his 401(k) ($17,500 deferred from his paycheck and $6,000 matched from his employer), and saves into his savings account ($500 per month), then his net worth will increase by the end of the year. And that doesn't even include the possible market appreciation of his home and/or return on his 401(k). By measuring his net worth, Marcus learns that he can move the financial needle by $49,500, or 5.7 percent of his net worth, at the beginning of the year.

Let's now examine the financial life of 42-year-old college professor Nancy.

January 1, 2014

Assets:	**$92,500**
Savings:	$3,500
403(b) Retirement Account:	$89,000
Debts:	**$25,000**
Medical bills:	$7,500
Credit cards:	$17,500
Net worth:	**$67,500**

Nancy isn't feeling too great about her financial state. Nancy never looks at her debts. They stress her out. "What's the point?" she often asks herself. But then Nancy decides to measure her activity for one year. She works hard to pay down her credit cards by $15,500. And she pays down $3,500 on her medical bills. Additionally, she starts contributing up to the match on her university's 403(b). Thus, she deposits $1,200, and the school matches $1,200. On December 31, Nancy does the math and realizes that she increased her net worth by $21,400, or a 31.7 percent increase. She's made amazing progress. And better yet, she's enthused. She's been working really hard on making financial changes, but she always felt like she was running in place. But she clearly isn't running in place: She improved her situation by more than 31 percent! That's phenomenal.

Can you imagine eating well, exercising regularly, feeling sad about your fitness progress, yet never weighing yourself to see whether you are getting any results? Yeah, it happens all the time—in exercise and in finance. When you don't measure your net worth, you miss the opportunity to reward your progress and hard work. Paying down debt can feel mundane, but it isn't. In fact, if you pay down $10,000 worth of debt, it has the same effect on your net worth as if you save $10,000. In both cases, it's a net worth increase of $10,000.

Do you want to start viewing your debt pay-down process differently? Then start measuring your net worth. The only debt I personally have is my mortgage, but I love figuring my net worth so I can measure the impact of my mortgage principal payments. I sincerely celebrate each mortgage payment, and so should you. The possibilities are endless when net worth is your go-to metric. Take for instance the story of pharmaceutical rep Brent.

Brent had lots of money. He was *consumed* with monitoring his portfolio's performance on a daily basis. Like many people, Brent lost sight of reality. He was so concerned with how well his broker was doing that he neglected to put any more of his income toward his investment portfolio. Instead, he chose to spend wildly because he had an $80,000 portfolio—even though, frankly, his portfolio was struggling. He lost 10 percent, or $8,000, in one year. The crazy thing is that Brent was completely wasting $1,500 per month on really stupid stuff. If Brent had monitored and utilized the net worth metric correctly, he would have increased his contributions to his portfolio by $18,000, despite his $8,000 loss. Not only would his net worth have increased, but he also would have hypothetically purchased more investments at a lower price, thus ensuring more profit once the portfolio turned around.

I love using net worth because it can reinvigorate individuals who've already amassed great wealth yet have fallen on apathetic times. It can refresh individuals who've dug themselves such a deep hole that they can't muster the fortitude to glance at their actual debt levels. I love using net worth to show anyone and everyone that purposeful financial decision-making will always lead to progress. As I said, net worth is the greatest financial metric in all of the financial world.

In practice, paying your debts is relatively simple compared to figuring out where your savings and investments should go. While there's a vast number of different investments, which we'll discuss in a moment, all the different types of savings and investments can go in one of three buckets.

THE THREE BUCKETS

To survive the present and plan for the future, you need to pay attention to three distinct segments of time: the now, the far off but sooner than you think, and the far off. You can address these three segments of time with three distinct buckets of money. These are more commonly known as your short-term savings, mid-term savings, and long-term savings. And believe it or not, there is a very specific way you need to build your savings into these three different buckets.

Even though Bucket #1 is your short-term savings, Bucket #2 is your mid-term savings, and Bucket #3 is your long-term savings, you don't want to start by putting money into Bucket #1. In fact, Bucket #3 gets your money first.

BUCKET #3

You always need to start by saving for your long-term financial goals. You need to employ the power of time as quickly as possible. It is your greatest ally when it comes to saving for the future. You must save into this bucket first, and in most instances you are saving into this bucket before your paycheck ever hits your checking account. And yes, you still need to save for the long term even when you are trying to pay off debt. Never stop contributing to this bucket. You will become so accustomed to it that you will forget you're doing it, and that's a good thing.

Under no circumstances can you wait to save for retirement. You must immediately defer a portion of your current income into your retirement savings. For many people, this means a 401(k), 403(b), or 401(a) that you access through your employer.

Waiting to save for the future is inexcusable for several reasons. First, you probably won't have three streams of retirement income like your parents and grandparents do or did. A pension, Social Security, and personal investments used to provide a diverse retirement-income strategy. But based on a few policy shifts and planning trends, only 15 percent of the private sector has a defined benefit plan (pension) today. You're more likely to have two streams of retirement income: Social Security and your own personal savings and investments.

Additionally, if you aren't saving into your company-sponsored retirement plan, you are likely missing out on the employer match. The employer match is when your employer contributes to your retirement plan based on your contributions to your retirement plan. They *match* your contribution up to a predetermined percentage.

If you don't have access to a retirement plan directly through your employer, you need to set up your own retirement plan. Depending on your situation, you may be eligible for a Roth IRA, a traditional IRA, a SIMPLE IRA, a SEP IRA, or even a solo 401(k). Your tax advisor can help you understand which plans you're eligible for and help you determine which plan is best for you. One of the main disadvantages of not having access to an employer-sponsored retirement plan is that you won't receive additional "free" compensation in the form of a match.

Once Bucket #3 is getting funded, it's on to Bucket #1.

BUCKET #1

Life happens. Whether this means your dog gets sick, your job is eliminated, or you need new tires on your car, at some point in the near future you're going to need money above and beyond your monthly income. I recommend having around $1,000 or so in this savings account while you are battling consumer debt (such as credit cards). The 10 percent allocation you'd otherwise put toward savings should be used for debt reduction when you have consumer debt. Once it's paid off, you can shift your focus back to saving.

Once your consumer debt is paid off, you need to accumulate three months' worth of expenses in your emergency fund. If your monthly expenses are $2,500, then you need $7,500 in your emergency fund. I know what you might be thinking: "That's a lot of money to have earning zero-point-nothing percent in interest." No it's not. This money is designed to have your back under any circumstances. You can't risk tying it up in illiquid investments or having it decrease in value by investing it in anything other than a savings account or a money market account. If $7,500 seems like a lot of money to you, your goal is to shift your thinking. Your emergency fund will decrease the financial stress in your life, and it will allow you to take additional risks with your mid-term bucket of money (which we'll discuss in a moment).

Before we move on, here are a couple of other rules for your emergency fund: It is not down payment money for a house. It is not new car money. It is for unexpected expenses. In fact, I'd prefer you use this account for almost any unexpected, involuntary expense. Brakes go out on your car? Use this money. Unexpected medical bill? Use this money. Stop trying to handle unusual expenses with your income. When you try to absorb an unusual expense without tapping into your savings, you end up throwing off your timing. Before you know it, your bills will be due before you get your next paycheck, and you'll wonder what happened. Use your emergency fund and then replenish it with your 10 percent monthly contribution to this savings. Once your short-term bucket is full, your future savings will go somewhere else. The key is that you never break the habit of saving. Your habit of saving will allow you put money into Bucket #2.

BUCKET #2

Once you've committed to saving for your retirement (by deferring money into your company-sponsored retirement plan), and once you've secured your present financial life (by saving three months' worth of expenses), then life can get really fun. If you thought spending and acquiring new things was fun, just wait until you get addicted to growth and accumulation.

When you've got more money than you know what to do with, you need to throw this money into the mid-term bucket. This mid-term bucket is technically called *nonqualified money*. This means it doesn't have any special tax advantage. The money doesn't grow tax deferred, but you don't have to wait until you are 59-1/2 to access the funds in this bucket (as long as you don't put money from this bucket into an annuity). Making regular contributions to this bucket certainly could warrant the need for a financial advisor. Since you've already filled up your emergency fund, you are cranking at least 10 percent (if not more) of your income into this mid-term bucket. The investments in this bucket need to fall in line with your risk tolerance, time horizon, and other financial considerations. These complexities are why I would like you to employ a financial advisor at this step in the process.

You're probably wondering what types of investments should go into this bucket. Well, lots of things could go into this bucket. Stocks, bonds, mutual funds, ETFs, real estate, or any other investment that doesn't lock up your money until you are 59-1/2 years old. However, you do need to be aware that some investments in this bucket can create current tax problems for you. Again, talk to a financial advisor or tax accountant about your particular situation.

And this is where things get really fun. You can use this bucket for anything. You can use it for a down payment on a home, a college education, a wedding, a vacation, a business, staying home with the kids for a predetermined amount of time, or anything else that tickles your fancy. If you want to enjoy life and not worry about money, then bust your hump to fill your emergency fund so that you can start putting money into this mid-term bucket.

Additionally, your goal is to crank up contributions to both the mid-term and the long-term buckets. Saving your raises helps with this, as does proper budgeting and an overall spirit of financial wellness. Now that you know the mechanics, it's time to learn more about the tools.

TYPES OF INVESTMENTS AND INVESTMENT VEHICLES

You may not aspire to be a brilliant investor, but you should aspire to understand investing. It's imperative that you understand certain terms and jargon of the financial industry. Every day of my life, I encounter people in their fifties and sixties who have no idea of the difference between a mutual fund and a stock. There is a difference, by the way, and it matters.

I don't know your current financial aptitude, so we'll start on the base level and work our way up to slightly more complicated concepts. If you understand the following terms, you'll be in good shape heading into your thirties.

STOCK

A stock is a share of the value of a company that can be purchased, sold, or traded as an investment. Although there are two main types of stocks—preferred stock and common stock—you're likely to be exposed only to common stock.

As an owner of preferred stock, you'll be among the first to receive dividends when the company either distributes extra cash during good times or liquidates assets during times of trouble. In addition, your dividend payout will be more consistent and predictable, as preferred stockholders are paid at regular intervals.

The same does not apply to common stockholders. As an owner of common stock, you'll receive payouts only when the company's board of directors approves a payout. You'll also be the last to receive dividends during liquidation, as companies must pay all preferred stockholders before they pay common stockholders.

Some stocks pay you, as a partial owner of the company, a portion of the profits. This disbursement is called a *dividend*. The dividend may be 30 to 40 cents per share, or it may be up to $3 or $4. You can reinvest these dividends into more shares of stock through things like Dividend Reinvestment Programs (DRIPs).

All in all, when you own stock in a company, you own a piece of the company—albeit a small piece.

BOND

A bond is an investment in which you serve as the lender—to a company, to a bank, or to the government. They borrow your money and promise to pay you back in full, with interest payments.

The more respectable the institution—such as the U.S. government or a large-scale corporation with a track record of long-term success—the safer the investment. With safer investments come lower interest rates and lower payouts. The riskier the loan, the more interest is up for grabs. You've probably heard the term *junk bond*. It refers to a bond that isn't rated very highly, yet pays a pretty handsome amount of interest. The risk for default (the bond being worth nothing) is higher, but the returns can be great, too. This fact alone can dispel the myth that bonds are collectively safe.

In addition, the duration of the bond plays into how lucrative it might be for you—the longer the duration of the bond period, the higher the payout.

In the end, when you buy a bond, you let an institution borrow your money.

MUTUAL FUND

A mutual fund is a collection of stocks and bonds managed by professional investors who diversify investments across a wide range of industries in an attempt to minimize risk. A mutual fund might contain investments in technology, agriculture, and pharmaceutical companies or any other industry, all in an attempt to ensure that the gains in one industry offset the losses in another.

Mutual funds earn income for you through the dividends on the stocks included in the fund and through interest from the bonds. If your stocks or bonds increase in price over the course of the year and your fund manager sells them at a higher price, the fund will experience a capital gain, the profits of which will be shared with investors.

EXCHANGE TRADED FUND

I should probably start by defining *index*. An index is a selection of stocks that are used to gauge the health and performance of the overall stock market. Whenever you hear or read "the market was up 38 points today," what they are talking about is the index. For instance, the Standard & Poor's 500 (S&P 500) Index is a group of 500 stocks that is used to measure the tone and direction of the stock market in general.

Exchange Traded Funds (ETFs) track the yields and returns of a specific index, such as the S&P 500 or the Dow Jones. Unlike other index funds, which try to beat the average performance of their index, an ETF attempts to mirror its index performance. In other words, if your Dow Jones ETF is performing exactly like the Dow Jones, it's doing well.

ETFs offer many of the same benefits of mutual funds—they're professionally managed and created to minimize risk—but the similarities end there. ETFs can be traded like a stock continually throughout the trading day, whereas mutual funds are priced only after the market closes. And because ETFs don't attempt to beat the market, they're less maintenance for managers, resulting in lower management fees.

As a result of these advantages, ETFs have become increasingly popular over the course of the last decade.

INDEX FUND

Index funds are similar to ETFs in that their success is tied to how well they replicate their index performance. For example, an index fund tracking the Dow Jones Industrial Average would own all of the same stocks as the Dow Jones.

Because index funds require minimal maintenance, they are passively managed. As a result, they have lower expense ratios (0.2 percent to 0.5 percent on average) than actively managed funds (which usually fall somewhere between 1.3 percent and 2.5 percent).

Index funds have grown in popularity both because of lower expense ratios and because market watchers realized that the indexes were outperforming mutual funds over the long term.

TARGET-DATE FUND

Target-date funds are investments that link investment selections with length of time from retirement. Each target-date fund is linked to a particular year—theoretically the year you wish to retire. Once you invest in this target-date fund, your investment allocation flows along what is called a *glide path*. This glide path consistently shifts the percentages of stock, bonds, and cash over time until they are at the "ideal" percentages to ready you for retirement. To add some additional complexity, a few target-date funds are meant to usher you through retirement, not just to retirement. The remainder of the target-date funds simply prepare your portfolio for retirement but aren't necessarily appropriate to hold when you are retired.

I've always thought of our investment allocations as cake recipes. Add the right amount of stock, the right amount of bonds, and the right amount of cash, and you will have a money-cake cooked to your liking. Target-date funds are prepackaged cakes. The ingredients are all right there, the cake is baked, and you can't adjust the recipe. Strangely, people mess up this part. If you have a target-date fund in your portfolio along with other funds, then you are basically pouring flour and/or sugar on the top of a prebaked cake that you just emptied into a mixing bowl from a plastic wrapper. Yeah, that's not going to taste good. When you combine a target-date fund with other investments in your account, you may create unintended consequences. Target-date funds were designed to be the only investment in your account.

If I were forced to rank investing strategies within a retirement plan, target-date funds would find themselves in third place. In first place, you'd find a relationship with an investment advisor who can help you make the right investment selections according to both your risk tolerance and your time horizon. Second place belongs to educating yourself and managing your investments in a suitable, unemotional way. Realistically, educating yourself and managing your investments in a suitable, unemotional way is intensely challenging. Sound investment strategy isn't built on guts and panache; it's built on discipline and patience. And while doing it yourself is the second-best option, it's the worst option if you don't know what you're doing.

Which brings us to third place. Target-date funds are perfect for individuals who don't have an investment advisor and don't take the time to thoroughly educate themselves on the principles of investing. Target-date funds generally have slightly higher fees than a la carte investments, but there's an obvious reason for that. They're alive! The investment allocations shift as you get closer to your target retirement date, and you don't have to do anything.

IRA

One of the more popular ways to save for retirement is through an Individual Retirement Account (IRA), also called a traditional IRA. You can put almost any type of investment inside of an IRA, including stocks, bonds, mutual funds, ETFs, and/ or index funds. Depending on your income, contributions to an IRA may be deductible on your income tax filing. They essentially have the same tax status as a 401(k). Additionally, an IRA allows your investments to grow without being subjected to capital gains or dividend income taxes. However, when you receive IRA distributions during retirement, your distributions will be considered income and will be subject to income tax.

An IRA is a popular choice for people who aren't offered an employer-sponsored retirement plan, such as a 401(k). A Roth IRA is also a popular option.

ROTH IRA

A Roth IRA is similar to a traditional IRA in that it allows you to direct part of your pre-tax income into investments intended to grow over time. However, where the traditional IRA is tax-deferred, meaning you don't pay taxes on the investment until it is distributed in retirement, the Roth IRA is taxed up front, and you don't have to pay taxes when you receive funds later.

And by later, I mean once you reach the age of 59-1/2.

401(k)

Most employers offer 401(k) plans as part of their compensation packages. A 401(k) enables you to make a contribution of each paycheck into a tax-deferred plan. Many employers offer a matching program, in which they will match your contribution up to a specified limit. So if the 401(k) match limit is 3 percent and you contribute 3 percent of your salary, your employer will match it, creating a total investment of 6 percent of your salary into your plan.

Needless to say, you should always save at least the maximum amount of your employer match, or you'll be leaving money on the table. And that's never a good thing.

529 COLLEGE SAVINGS PLAN

Qualified tuition programs—or 529s, as most people call them—were created under the Small Business Job Protection Act of 1996. They work a lot like Roth IRAs in terms of taxation, but 529 plans are designed to help you save for a college education. It can be your college education or your child's college education. It doesn't really matter.

Every state has its own 529 College Savings Plan. You can invest your money in any of them. You don't have to go to school or live in the state of the plan in which you invest, either. Many people, myself included, choose the 529 plan in the state in which they live because of the state tax benefits. However, every state has different ways in which it incentivizes or doesn't incentivize depositors to save for college. Although fees and investment performance are certainly important factors in making your 529 selection, state tax benefits are hard to pass up. If your state has allowed for tax credits or anything else of the sort in relation to depositing into a 529 College Savings Plan, you should explore it thoroughly before looking to another state's plan.

ANNUITY

Some financial products don't make much sense to consider until a certain age. An annuity is such a product. Now, don't get upset if you have an annuity through your employer as part of your retirement plan. That's different. For the sake of the following discussion, when I refer to an annuity, I'm referring to an insurance product that you buy directly from an insurance company.

Annuities do many things, but one of their primary functions can make them impractical if you're younger. When you put money into an annuity, the money is "locked up" until you turn 59-1/2. An annuity turns your money into tax-deferred money. This means you won't pay taxes on the growth the annuity receives until you withdraw the money after age 59-1/2. That's right, you can't withdraw money from an annuity prior to age 59-1/2 without a tax penalty. Depending on what you're intending your annuity to do for you, turning your investment into a chunk of money you can't touch until you turn 59-1/2 isn't necessarily a bad thing.

When you invest in an annuity, you give your money to a life insurance company that attempts to grow your money. The life insurance company helps mitigate the risks associated with investing, whether by guaranteeing returns or by guaranteeing fixed payments to you at a later date for a set period of time.

Many people utilize annuities to ensure a steady stream of income during retirement. There are two primary ways in which an annuity can provide retirement income: annuitization or withdrawals. When you annuitize an annuity, you give up rights to the principal to receive fixed lifetime monthly payments. While giving up access to a giant chuck of money doesn't exactly sound fun, it can actually make sense in certain instances.

Annuities have the reputation for being expensive. It is true that annuities can be much more expensive than mutual funds and ETFs, but the reason for the added expense is that there are typically guarantees associated with annuities. By the nature of the fact that life insurance is involved, the additional expense purchases risk mitigation from the insurance company. You just need to decide how much you are willing to pay to receive a set of guarantees.

If you choose to go the annuity route, make sure you understand what exactly the fees are buying you. There are three primary types of annuities, and each one comes with its own unique set of fees. The first type of annuity, a fixed annuity, is pretty straightforward. Your fees will be primarily limited to mortality and expense charges—or M&Es, as industry people call them. They are called *fixed annuities* because you will typically receive a fixed rate on your investment principal.

Index annuities are the second primary type of annuity. These types of annuities are linked to market indexes and are meant to allow you to participate in the upside of the market and then protect you from market downswings. In doing so, your gains are typically capped. For instance, your cap may be 8 percent.

This means if the market (usually the S&P 500) increases in value by 20 percent in a particular year, then your gains would be limited to just 8 percent. However, if the market were to fall 20 percent, you generally wouldn't take any loss at all. Your annuity wouldn't be credited with any gains during the down years, but you also wouldn't lose a penny. The "capped" nature of index annuities is what can make them seem expensive. If the market does 20 percent and you get 8, one might argue that you paid a 12 percent fee.

A variable annuity is far and away the most complicated type. It can involve both significant risk and significant expense. That doesn't make it bad, but you should take the time to fully understand *all* of the moving pieces of a variable annuity before purchasing one. The expenses within a variable annuity can approach 4 percent annually, once you figure in the expenses for each individual investment within the plan. It's very common to purchase riders on all types of annuities, especially variable annuities. A rider is a bell and whistle, if you will. It enhances the annuity by guaranteeing various elements of the plan. For example, a rider may guarantee that your variable annuity grows at no less than 5 percent per year, or it may guarantee that you can take extra income off of the annuity if you are in a long-term-care facility.

As you approach your late forties, annuities may begin to come into focus as you look to guarantee retirement income sources. But if they do, take your time, do the math, and make sure the fees and the fact that you lock up your money until 59-1/2 don't prevent them from being a good idea.

WHY YOU CAN'T WAIT TO INVEST

What people fail to understand is that when you don't save for the future, you can't use time as a tool. When your money grows, it (ideally) grows every year. For instance, if you invest $5,000 that earns 8 percent, then after one year you will have $5,400. Great. But if you make this initial investment 20 years from your retirement goal versus five years from your retirement goal, then time makes all the difference.

Take a look at the following table. Let's say you are 45 years old, and you decide to invest $5,000 per year for just five years and leave the money alone for 20 years from the day of the initial investment. And let's assume that you earn an 8 percent rate of return on your money. This is a very reasonable rate of return over a 20-year period. Obviously, you would need to be in some sort of stock market investment (stocks, ETFs, or mutual funds) to receive that sort of return. At the end of 20 years, you would have $100,493.19. Not too shabby.

Now, let's assume you wait to start investing until you are 60 years old. Even if you saved three times the amount of money ($15,000) each year for five years, you still wouldn't be able to equal the account that started growing at age 45. Money isn't the issue here; time is the issue.

People tend to think they will have more money to save when they get older. This may or may not be true. But even if it is true, those people will need to save three times the amount if they want to achieve the exact same financial goals. Would you like to invest $25,000 to reach $100,000? Or would you rather invest $75,000?

Time in Years	Investment	Growth	Investment	Growth
1	$5,000.00	$5,400.00		
2	$5,000.00	$11,232.00		
3	$5,000.00	$17,530.56		
4	$5,000.00	$24,333.00		
5	$5,000.00	$31,679.65		
6		$34,214.02		
7		$36,951.14		
8		$39,907.23		
9		$43,099.81		
10		$46,547.79		
11		$50,271.62		
12		$54,293.34		
13		$58.636.81		
14		$63,327.76		
15		$68,393.98		
16		$73,865.50	$15,000.00	$16,200.00
17		$79,774.74	$15,000.00	$33,696.00
18		$86,156.71	$15,000.00	$52,591.68
19		$93,049.25	$15,000.00	$72,999.01
20		$100,493.19	$15,000.00	$95,038.94

Additional complexities appear when you wait to start investing for the future. As you get closer toward your hypothetical goal of having $100,000 by age 65, you are forced to take more risk because you need your money to grow unnaturally fast. Conversely, the further you are away from your goal of having $100,000 by age 65, the less risk you have to take. You could invest less than $5,000 initially at age 45 and still hit your $100,000 goal if you continued investing after the fifth year. You could invest $100,000 on your 65th birthday and hit your goal, too.

The next time you hear or think that there's plenty of time to invest, you need to check yourself. There's plenty of time for your money to grow, but the longer you wait to invest, the harder it will be.

ONE MORE NOTE ON THE MATCH

I've referenced "the match" a few different times now. The match is what your employer is willing to contribute to your retirement plan, based on what you contribute to your retirement plan. For instance, if you contribute 3 percent of your annual income to your retirement plan, your employer may match your contribution by also contributing 3 percent to your retirement plan. This is free money

And while the match is great, unfortunately people have become obsessed with it. "Pete, I hit the match!" Okay, enough. That's great. You are supposed to hit your match. How much time should I spend celebrating your unwillingness to ignore extra compensation opportunities?

Hitting the match is as elementary as brushing your teeth. Brushing your teeth isn't a goal; you just do it. Hitting the match isn't a goal; you just do it. You're probably wondering what's beyond the match. If I'm asking you to somewhat dismiss the importance of the match, then I must be asking you to do something in addition to the match. You are correct. But we need to continue to get weirder for a moment.

"Pete, I put 10 percent of my income into my retirement plan!" Okay. Why? "Well, I figure it's a round number, and it just seems to make sense." Yes, it is a round number, and no, it doesn't make sense. Why would a round number make sense? Your retirement plan will be used to replace your income when you retire. What do round numbers have to do with anything?

Your goal isn't to live in a world of round numbers and cute rules of thumb. Your goal is to be able to stop working someday. Ask yourself, what in the world will saving 5 percent or 10 percent of your income do for you, come retirement time? Nothing. It will do nothing. I don't say this to kill your buzz or ruin your day. Because your retirement will be different from your parents' and grandparents' retirement, based on the number of retirement income sources, your retirement will be possible only if you break your dependency on your income and defer tremendous amounts of money into your retirement plan.

You've probably noticed that the term *financial independence* is used often to describe retirement. Financial independence is meant to describe our lack of dependence on work income. But in a very strange twist, most financial independence (retirement) planning does very little to break income dependency. It really only focuses on accumulating more and more money. Where'd the independence go?

You can create independence by deferring as much money as possible into your retirement plan. In 2014, you could defer $17,500 of your income into your company-sponsored retirement plan (because you are under 50 years old). Your goal is to do that. I'm not kidding. To think your retirement will go well without it is shortsighted. Here's an example:

If you were to save $17,500 every year, starting today, for 35 years, at an 8 percent rate of return, you'd end up with $3,015,544.

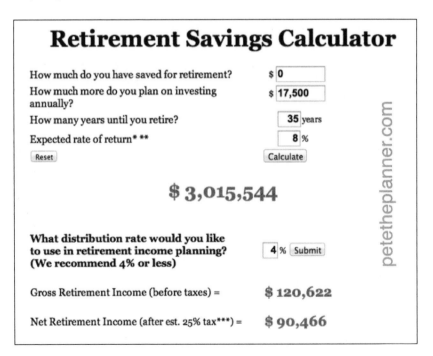

If you were to distribute 4 percent of that money to yourself in retirement (4 percent is widely considered to be the amount of money you should withdraw from your retirement investments on an annual basis), you'd receive $120,622 per year gross. Great, huh? Well, you have to pay taxes. Let's estimate a 25 percent effective tax rate. That brings your net income to $90,466. What's that? You're wondering about inflation? Me too. If money loses half of its buying power every 25 years or so, then your $90,466 is going to feel more like $40,000 in today's dollars. Yes, I made lots of assumptions, and contribution limits and tax brackets will change. But the point of this is to give you a general idea of what you're up against. By the way, feel free to use our retirement calculator to run your own scenarios at PeteThePlanner.com/Retirement-Calculator.

What if you contributed $8,000 per year?

Retirement Savings Calculator

How much do you have saved for retirement?	$ 0
How much more do you plan on investing annually?	$ 8,000
How many years until you retire?	35 years
Expected rate of return* **	8 %

Reset   Calculate

$ 1,378,534

What distribution rate would you like to use in retirement income planning? (We recommend 4% or less)   4 % Submit

Gross Retirement Income (before taxes) =   **$ 55,141**

Net Retirement Income (after est. 25% tax***) =   **$ 41,356**

petetheplanner.com

Looks like your inflation-adjusted retirement income will be less than $20,000 per year. You can't expect to continue your current financial lifestyle, within reason, if you don't put good money away for the future.

The biggest complaint I hear in this regard is "Pete, your retirement savings expectations are unrealistic. Who can afford to save that much?" There's a ton of failed thinking with this complaint. Here's what I know: If you don't save this money, you won't be able to have a reasonable retirement. I know that $3 million and $1.3 million seems like a lot of money, but 35 years from now, it'll be a lot less than you think. Additionally, if you get frisky and distribute your assets at a rate higher than 4 percent, then you risk running out of money.

This chart is a Monte Carlo simulation from my book *Mock Retirement*. It's based on a 60 percent stock and 40 percent bond asset mix during retirement. I ran 5,000 simulations using historical market data to determine the success rate of your retirement for different distribution rates. If you think an 8 percent chance of failure is no big deal, ask yourself whether you would get on a train if the conductor announced prior to leaving the station, "This train has an 8 percent chance of crashing. Enjoy the ride!" I'd be off that death train faster than you could possibly imagine.

Retirement doesn't feel real for anyone who's 15 years or more from retirement. Because of this, we don't really do the math. And the further out we are from retirement, the more we depend on something mystical to happen to change our financial future. Mystical things don't happen to change our financial paths. Your retirement will only work if you dismiss the glory of your match. Your goal is to max out your retirement

60 Percent Stock / 40 Percent Bond

Percent of Portfolio Used per Year	10 Years	15 Years	20 Years	25 Years	30 Years
3.00%	100%	100%	100%	100%	99%
3.50%	100%	100%	100%	98%	96%
4.00%	100%	100%	99%	96%	92%
4.50%	100%	100%	97%	92%	86%
5.00%	100%	100%	94%	85%	79%
5.50%	100%	98%	90%	79%	69%
6.00%	100%	96%	83%	69%	59%
6.50%	100%	92%	75%	60%	48%
7.00%	100%	87%	65%	52%	41%
7.50%	99%	81%	58%	41%	30%
8.00%	98%	74%	47%	32%	23%
8.50%	96%	66%	38%	24%	18%
9.00%	94%	57%	32%	18%	12%

plan, not hit some silly match that tricks you into thinking you are doing something about your retirement problem.

If for some reason your employer doesn't have a company-sponsored retirement plan, then set up an IRA or a Roth IRA on your own. The limits on IRAs and Roth IRAs are much lower than a company-sponsored retirement plan, but these contribution limits generally increase over time.

SAVING FOR COLLEGE

Whether it's retirement planning or trying to pay for your child's education, waiting to invest is obviously a mistake. You may know very well the ill effects of student loans. Then again, if you continued your education after high school, your parents may very well have paid for it. Either way, if you have children, you need to make a decision on how you plan to address their potential college costs.

Whether your child is 10 months old or 10 years old, you must develop a personal philosophy regarding your perceived obligation to fund your child's education and you must act on said philosophy. It's up to you to decide whether you are going to participate in your children's college funding. It truly is a personal choice. However, the choice isn't inaction. Don't forego the very important step of deciding how you are going to handle their college costs. Unfortunately, when you don't make a conscious decision one way or another, the default selection is student loans.

Whether you like it or not, in the eyes of the federal government, you are at least partially responsible for paying for your adult child's education (if your child is 18 to 23 years old). This has long been the case. The Department of Education, colleges and universities, and the rest of the federal government also need you to know that if students want to borrow money on their own to fund their education without the help of their parents, the parents will still likely be required to fund a portion of the education. This is all to say that if you don't save for your child's college, then you are likely to be forced—yes, *forced*—to pay for some of their college once they get there. You will need to pay with other assets, cash-flow the expenses as they arrive, or the worst option of all, take out Parent PLUS loans. Parent PLUS loans are student loans that parents take out for their child's education. Parent PLUS loans are increasingly popular, and they are increasingly responsible for destroying retirement planning.

HIRING A FINANCIAL ADVISOR

Financial advisors are like wine. A higher price point doesn't always equal better results. On top of that, as with wine, personal preference and tastes can dictate the consumer's experience and satisfaction. Every person in the world besides you may like a particular wine, but if you don't like it, what's the point of drinking it? You need to understand how your priorities, attitude, and personality intersect with a potential advisor's offerings.

How do you select the right financial advisor? It's a very simple question that elicits stress, fear, and confusion in the average financial consumer. And it's a question that I never fully understood until I stopped working with personal financial planning clients. From the outset, the process of selection is overwhelming. Consider the titles alone. How would you even begin to decipher the following jargon?

Financial planner. Investment planner. Investment advisor. Financial consultant. Financial advisor. Registered representative. Financial specialist. Agent. Retirement planner. College planner. Broker.

In the words of my precocious four-year-old, "Good luck with that."

And if you make the right title choice, you'll next need to decide what you want out of an advisor relationship. If you choose to hire a financial advisor, you should expect the person to serve two primary functions. First, your advisor should help you find and evaluate investment opportunities. Second, your advisor should move you forward financially. Your net worth should increase. This means that your debts should decrease and your savings and investments should increase. While these are the reasons to hire a good financial advisor, you'll still need to make sense of who to hire.

You really only need a financial advisor if you are going to invest. It has been my experience that financial advisors offer very little expertise in anything other than investing and technical financial planning. By the way, debt and budgeting generally fall outside this expertise. A good financial advisor will be important to your future. Once you've cleaned up all your debt, budgeting issues, and discipline issues, like we all have to, then follow these tips to pick a great financial advisor.

▶ **Knowledge.** It's even weird to write about this. A great majority of financial-industry people have no idea what they're doing. In fact, in 2012 a cat named Orlando outperformed a number of investment advisors in the U.K. And no, I don't mean cat as in he was a cool cat. I mean he had whiskers and drank out of a saucer. Orlando threw his toy on a grid filled with different options. Where his toy landed, is where the money was invested. The cat dominated the experts who were using "traditional" means. And I by traditional means I mean no batting a cat toy across a grid of investments.

No one knows what the market is going to do. No one. They might have a theory as to why it might go up or down, but they don't actually know. Financial advisors love to compare themselves to doctors, but I hope that doctors don't guess as much as financial advisors do. This isn't meant to be overcritical; it's just fact. You simply want your financial advisor to position you in the best possible manner so that you can do well in good markets and survive in bad markets. Anyone else that tells you they can do something different from this is lying. Come to think of it, this first quality should probably be "humility paired with knowledge." Your financial advisor should be able to give you confidence via his or her vulnerability. Several financial advisors try to gain your confidence by appearing all-knowing. That's a bad idea, especially if a cat named Orlando just beat their returns.

▶ **Attentiveness.** No one likes to be ignored. I've accidentally neglected to return phone calls. I've accidentally neglected to return emails. Does this mean I'm terrible at customer service? To some, it may seem that way. The reality is that no matter the industry, customer service is really important, yet at times people make mistakes. When money is involved—all the money you have ever saved—things can get extra stressful when a phone call isn't returned. You'll know if your advisor is ducking you. You should meet with your advisor at least once per year, and the responsibility for setting up this meeting is shared.

▶ **Ability to teach.** Do you know what an American Depositary Receipt (ADR) is? No? That's okay; you wouldn't be in the minority. If you work with a good advisor for long enough, you will learn stuff like this and be better for it. I tend to eat at restaurants that make me a better home cook. Somehow, some way, I learn things about cooking by interacting with the waitstaff or kitchen staff. Have you been with a financial advisor for five years, yet you haven't learned anything? That's bad. Make sure you are a better investor for having known the advisor you're working with.

▶ **Risk radar.** Do you want to hear something crazy but true? I became a riskier investor, personally, when I stopped investing other people's money. Weird, right? I don't think so. My theory is that I never wanted my personal risk tolerance, derived from years of study and experience, to bleed over into my clients' risk tolerance. It'd be like trying to convince someone to like spicy food, despite the fact that it gives them ulcers. If you don't want to take risks with your money, then don't. My least favorite thing about the investment industry is that if your advisor is wrong, then you are the one who suffers. You should dictate the direction of your investments by allowing the advisor to thoroughly measure your risk tolerance.

▶ **Reasonable fees.** Did you notice that I didn't say *fee only* or *commission only*? Why? Because, frankly, I've learned that it doesn't matter. The theory in the fee-based financial planning community (advisors that charge either a flat rate or a percentage of your assets invested) is that the only way to ensure objective advice is to limit compensation to the fee-based method. This is a fallacy. A commission salesperson isn't inherently biased. Would you rather have a commission-based financial advisor who knows what he or she is doing or a fee-based advisor who simply passed a test? Compensation structure is not a tell. You can't smoke out a crook by looking only at how someone is compensated. Some of the top Ponzi schemes of all time were perpetrated by fee-based advisors (Bernie Madoff). Just make sure your advisor has reasonable fees. And we'll leave it at that.

Here's the crazy thing about these five qualities: Everyone will measure them differently, just like wine. Some of my past clients may have thought I struggled at any one, if not all, of the qualities listed above. And because it's their perspective and their perspective alone, they'd be right. This is why advisor ratings—and wine ratings, for that matter—should be taken

Chapter 7 ◆ The Piggy Bank: Saving and Investing

with a grain of salt. I've always thought advisor ratings were silly. I was once ranked as a top advisor at one of the firms I worked for. The rankings were based on production and nothing else. I was rated as excellent because I produced a lot of revenue for the firm, not because I was objectively good. Oddly enough, I've seen several advisors at the top of several companies leave the industry due to ethical and disciplinary issues. On top of that, many advisor ratings are linked to advertising buys.

This is why you should interview potential advisors and not just blindly go with the person a friend recommends. I love my friends, but I hate some of their wine recommendations. Do your best to try to evaluate these five qualities during your interview. My bottom line is this: You should be treated how you want to be treated by someone who knows what they're doing, all the while understanding your risk tolerance and charging you moderate fees.

But maybe the bigger point is this: You need to clean up your habits before you bother with an investment advisor, anyway.

FEES FOR A FINANCIAL ADVISOR

The financial planning industry has a practical, yet insincere solution to the advisor selection quandary. The people in the industry have decided to turn the question into one of compensation. This path makes some sense, yet it offers close to zero solutions for those people without investable assets. In other words, if you don't have copious amounts of money to invest, then you will be passed over by the industry ethicists, the fee-based advisors, and fee-only advisors. This is where the confusion really begins.

There are primarily three ways in which financial advisors are compensated: commission-based, fee-based, and fee-only.

A commission-based advisor doesn't charge fees, but instead is compensated by investment and insurance companies upon selling their investments to consumers. And as crazy as this sounds, commission-based advisors have no industry-regulated responsibility to do what's in the client's best interest. This is called *fiduciary responsibility*, and commission-based advisors don't have it. Is a commission-based advisor predestined to give you biased financial advice based on potential commission rates? Arguably, but not always. Some experts argue that human nature prevents commission-based advisors from giving objective financial advice. I disagree.

A fee-based advisor charges a fee to manage investment assets and can still accept commissions from insurance and investment companies, whereas a fee-only advisor collects a fee for managing your money but doesn't accept any commission from third parties. The idea is to create an objective environment of fiduciary responsibility. However, the assertion that a fee-based or fee-only advisor is undeniably scrupulous is absurd. You do realize that speed-limit signs aren't suggestions, right? The main problem with this method is the imposition of "minimum assets" policies.

For a moment, let's say you have $8,000 to your name. Is that a lot of money? If you only have $8,000, then it's a tremendous amount of money. In fact, it's 100 percent of your money. Do you want it invested wisely? Yes. Do you want it invested in an unbiased way? Yes. Do you want someone to pick up the phone when you call to find someone to invest your money? Yes. The only person likely to pick up the phone is going to be a commission-based advisor.

This is a problem that the industry has created. The industry has basically said, "If you have $50,000 to invest, then we've got several ways in which the industry can objectively serve you." That doesn't work for me. Fee-based and fee-only advisors typically have minimum client requirements. I don't begrudge businesspeople's right to make business decisions on who they want or don't want as clients, but the scrutiny being placed on commission-based advisors for taking on smaller clients is unjust. This is all to say that picking your advisor based on how they're compensated is popular and convenient, but overrated.

No matter what type of advisor you choose, you owe it to yourself and your money to do a broker check. A broker check will allow you to see the regulatory history of your advisor. You'll be able to see complaints, judgments, and interesting patterns. Should you then make your judgment solely on what you find on the advisor's broker check? Nope. But I wouldn't consider hiring an advisor without first running a broker check. You can run a check on your advisor at BrokerCheck.FINRA.org.

EVALUATING YOUR FINANCIAL ADVISOR

Is your financial advisor performing well? It's a very simple question. It's so simple that it's actually kind of challenging to answer. In a perfect world, financial advisors would tell you exactly how to evaluate their performance, and some actually do this. And some advisors want you to hire them for the same reason they don't want you to fire them. That reason? Performance.

Let's change industries for a moment. If you were to hire a painter to paint your house, how would you determine whether the person did an acceptable job? I'm sure there are many ways, but they all boil down to results: You want to see results. I'm sure you might lose some sleep if the person didn't call you back and/or communicate with you appropriately, but ultimately you care about the paint on the house. Does the painter have to be smarter than everyone else? Does the painter need to pick some obscure paint that he designed himself? Would you keep a very personable painter who does a terrible paint job? There's a standard way to measure results: The paint needs to be on the house without streaks, and that's pretty much it.

There are a ridiculous number of ways to measure the performance of any individual you hire, but the end result is the most important thing. As much as I want to think 50 different things matter when evaluating a financial advisor, only two things really matter. Don't get me wrong: I want the person to communicate brilliantly with you, remember your birthday, and know financial and tax laws. But if your advisor does everything right except the following two things, is he or she really doing a good job?

▶ **Performance in relation to the index.** If your advisor can't consistently beat the index, what's the point of paying for management fees? I realize there are several investment objectives to consider, but if your objective is growth and the advisor's recommendations don't beat the S&P 500, then why not just invest in an index fund that replicates the S&P 500?

This is where you start to learn the differences between active and passive management. An index fund is a passive investment that has the same holdings as a given stock market index. A stock market index is used to judge and evaluate a particular portion of the market. There isn't a Svengali pushing buttons and pulling levers. The stocks or bonds within an index fund don't change frequently. Nothing is sold at highs or bought at lows. As my daughter says, "You get what you get, and you won't throw a fit."

Actively managed funds are the opposite of this. The positions (stocks and bonds) within the fund can change with varying degrees of frequency. The goal is to buy low and sell high. Investment professionals use either fundamental analysis or technical analysis to decide what will or won't make money. As you can imagine, all of this activity (analyzing, buying, and selling) costs money. So not only does your advisor need the actively managed fund to beat the passively managed index, but he or she also needs the actively managed fund to beat the passive fund by the amount of fees you are paying on the active funds. In other words, the fees must justify better performance. Otherwise, by this performance measure, you should just buy an index fund.

Every investment strategy is an educated guess. Yes, an educated guess. Unless you are buying a product with a guaranteed rate, you are putting your money at risk. And even guaranteed-rate investments have their risks. Your advisor also measures the amount of risk he or she takes against the index. Your tolerance for risk will dictate how aggressive your investments are in relation to the index. It's quite possible that you don't have the risk tolerance needed to invest in even an S&P 500 index fund. If this is the case, then you shouldn't bust your advisor's chops if he or she can't beat the index, because in this instance the index has a different risk level. Your risk tolerance and time horizon should be important factors your advisor uses to create your investment portfolio.

I may be in the minority, but I think the most important thing a financial advisor can do is convince you to invest a portion of your income. An advisor should make a compelling case as to why he or she should have your income instead of you. This isn't as nefarious as it may seem. So many clients and advisors get caught up in what to do about current investable assets. In other words, everyone involved cares way too much about money that has already been saved. Don't get me wrong—you shouldn't jack around with money you've already saved. Your advisor will prove her worth by how she invests your already saved assets. But your advisor will prove she's worth a darn by tapping your most valuable asset: your income.

Think of every financial billboard, commercial, or print ad you have ever seen. What do a majority of them say? It's my experience that a majority of them say, "We can help you with your rollover"—meaning they can help you invest your old retirement plan. Or, they can help you invest money you've already saved. Great! Who couldn't do that? A great financial advisor will emphasize the importance of saving your current income, not just invest the money you've already saved.

Does she get paid nearly as much to invest your current income? No. Therefore, the second measure of how to determine whether your financial advisor is worth her *fleur de sel* is whether you accomplished anything financial with your current income.

▶ **Performance in relation to your income being used toward your financial goals.** I'm not suggesting I just discovered electricity here, but I'm pretty sure this is a brilliant measure. Did your advisor convince you, with all her knowledge, degrees, and tools, that she has a workable plan for a portion of your income? And if she convinced you, did you give it to her and accomplish anything? If you can say yes to both of these questions, I would argue that you have a heck of an advisor. The financial industry likes to argue with itself about whether it's a sales industry. It is. The sale occurs when the advisor, with all her esoteric insider know-how, sells you on the concept that your income is valuable. I don't care how an advisor is compensated or whether she thinks she's in sales, her job is to sell you on the idea that you should use your current income to accomplish your financial goals.

If your current advisor hasn't ever addressed the use of your income, then what is she really doing? Is she simply weighing in on the money you've already saved? What value is that? An index fund could do that. I firmly believe you should measure your financial advisor based on how much or how little she addresses your current income. Some of this money will be used to buy life insurance, but a vast majority of this income should be used to save for emergencies, your kids' college, and/or your retirement.

► Or, there is one other option. One option so outlandish that you know it's good. Your advisor can help you use your income to reduce your debts. You see, if advisors were significantly involved in your personal finances, then they would be able to not only convince you, but also motivate you to pay down your consumer debt. Your net worth calculation proves this. If your advisor convinces and motivates you to pay off $5,000 in consumer debt, then she's had the same effect on your net worth as convincing you to save or invest $5,000.

An additional note: You are stubborn. Don't take offense at this. You are. We all are. If you don't save money or pay off debt, it's your own fault, not your advisor's. But there are financial advisors that can help you see the light, while others just use a truckload of color laser cartridges to print 60-page plans that never see the light of day. Your advisor is a crucial person in your life. If he or she isn't, then you might not have a good one. You can evaluate your advisor via market performance and you-based performance. And if your advisor can't beat the market, he or she sure better be able to beat your income out of you.

RISK

Every person decides how much risk he or she is willing to deal with. What most people don't realize is that a person can't actually avoid risk. When people attempt to mitigate risk, they often expose themselves to different types of risk. This is especially true when it comes to financial planning.

Before we discuss some of the lesser-known financial risks, let's examine how someone arrives at his personal risk tolerance. Simply put, risk tolerance is a measure of how much risk a person is willing to accept in order to pursue investment returns. A low risk tolerance generally means a person isn't willing to have his or her savings or investments decrease in value due to market activity. On the other hand, a person with a high risk tolerance is willing to accept fluctuations in account values, even when account values dip into the negative. The biggest drivers of risk tolerance are personal experience and philosophy, knowledge level, and time horizon.

Nothing destroys a moderate risk tolerance quite like an investment portfolio getting hammered. Even if the investments were suitable, reasonable, and appropriate, investment loss can significantly affect a person's willingness to take future risk, even if and when the portfolio rises again. A negative experience can make people more introspective and conservative with their money.

I believe the number-one factor in determining risk tolerance is knowledge. People fear things they don't understand, as they should. If someone doesn't understand investments and the financial markets, frankly, they shouldn't proceed with investing anyway. The better solution would be to hire a trusted financial advisor, paired with a purposeful strategy to learn more about how the market works. If people don't know what they are doing, refuse to hire an advisor, and refuse to increase their financial education level, then they should have a low risk tolerance. It's self-preservation. It's necessary.

The final factor in determining risk tolerance is time horizon. Risk tolerance and time horizon have a very important relationship. As a person gets closer to the need for saved money, time horizon shrinks, and risk tolerance will almost always decrease. For example, when you're 30 years out from retirement, you may have a higher risk tolerance than you would when you are 30 days out from retirement. Some people struggle to make wise retirement planning decisions because they don't account for time horizon. Instead, they make their investment decisions solely based on their long-developed risk tolerance. In my opinion, this is a mistake. My theory on risk is simple: Never take an ounce of market risk more than you need to in order to accomplish your goal. I believe both risk tolerance and time horizon are factors in making this decision.

And then there are the numbers. When doing some research for a retirement book, I learned that taking market risk makes a significant impact on retirement. Based on 5,000 simulations of a retirement scenario using historical market returns, a person with a portfolio of 50 percent bond, 30 percent cash, and 20 percent stock has an 89 percent chance of having money left over after taking annual withdrawals of 4 percent (of total portfolio value) for 30 years. A person who has a 100 percent cash portfolio (money market and savings), has a 19 percent chance of having any money left over, using the same withdrawal schedule. This makes the case that conservative investors often hurt themselves with conservative portfolio construction.

No one should invest against his or her risk tolerance. If you are a conservative investor, you are a conservative investor. There is no shame in that game. You shouldn't let anyone talk you out of being a conservative investor. The statistics above shouldn't even talk you out of being a conservative investor. Feel free to educate yourself on the markets and investing, but if that doesn't make you feel less conservative, then don't change unless you're willing to accept the risk.

DEALING WITH REALITY

Now that you've addressed debt, learned to budget, learned about making major purchases, discussed credit, and learned about savings and investing, it's time to have a very uncomfortable talk. Sometimes life goes extra wrong, in spite of all your diligence and planning. For those moments, you can turn to one place: insurance.

CHAPTER 8

THE PITFALLS: INSURANCE

Do you remember your twenties, when you arguably had nothing to lose? Good. Now forget about that. Because in your forties, you have a ton to lose. You are in the middle of your career, your family structure may be as complicated as ever, and you may have just enough money to foolishly convince yourself that you're bulletproof.

Insurance isn't just practical at this point in your life, it's necessary. Insurance protects your assets from a liability perspective, in relation to both your actions and the actions of the rest of your family. Yes, I'm talking about the possibility that you may have a teen driver.

It's possible that you are within a decade of eliminating your need for a few different types of insurance. Retirement preparation does that. When your retirement plan is fully funded and ready to pay out, you may be able stop paying premiums on both life insurance and disability insurance. That's good news, right? Well, kinda.

First, dropping your life insurance and/or disability insurance is prudent only when you become somewhat self-insured. In other words, you have accumulated enough money that the impact of your death or disability becomes financially insignificant. And second, not only will your insurance needs shift you *out of* some products, but also your needs will shift you *into* some products. You are just a few years away from exploring and possibly purchasing long-term care insurance. Don't worry about that now, but just know it's coming.

At this point in your life, you should be primarily concerned with a few different types of insurance: health insurance, car insurance, renters or homeowners insurance, disability insurance, and life insurance. Of course, you may not need one or two of these coverages, but it's probably not the ones you think. Regardless of whether you are single, you will still need life insurance and disability insurance. The coverages you may be exempt from are auto insurance if you don't have a vehicle, and either homeowners or renters insurance if you don't own a home or don't rent, respectively.

CONSIDER GETTING AN INSURANCE AGENT

Buying insurance over the phone or Internet is as popular as ever, but that doesn't mean it's the right thing to do. Can you save a few bucks by buying coverage through a call center? Sure. Can that same call center be there when you have questions? Sure. But you are paying a ton of money for insurance across the board. You deserve to fully understand your coverage, and you deserve to have an advocate. I don't want to talk to a different person every time I have an insurance question. I want a reliable and constant source of information and assistance.

A personal relationship with an insurance agent is a great relationship to have. Not to trivialize relationships based on utility, but an insurance agent is an amazing tool to have when emergencies arrive.

Although your insurance agent can point you in the right direction for most of your insurance needs, you still need to have a base level of understanding of each type of insurance.

TYPES OF INSURANCE

Here's what you need to know about each type of insurance coverage at this point in your life. Additionally, you'll find a few pointers on how to make each of these coverages work even better for you and your financial goals.

HEALTH

Fortunately for you, the trend in healthcare today points consumers to what is called *consumer-driven healthcare*. It's a concept that not only protects you, it also rewards you for low-risk behavior. It consists of a health savings account (HSA), paired with a high-deductible health insurance plan. I've come to the conclusion that an HSA is a great decision, especially for those who are not only healthy but also fiscally responsible. And given that you're reading a book about how to be financially responsible, it may be the perfect strategy for you.

The key is the HSA. Instead of putting all of your budgeted money toward a traditional health insurance plan that features co-pays, prescription drug coverage, and relatively low deductibles, an HSA paired with a high-deductible health insurance plan splits money into two pots. The first pot of money is used to pay for your health insurance coverage. The second pot of money is deposited into your HSA, where it sits until you have healthcare costs. Don't have any healthcare costs? Then keep the money in your HSA. The money that is in your HSA will always be yours, and it has no expiration date in terms of use.

In traditional health insurance, you may have co-pays for doctor's office visits and prescriptions, none of which typically go toward your overall deductible. However, when using an HSA paired with a high-deductible health insurance plan, you pay for all medical expenses until you reach your deductible.

You pay for prescriptions, procedures, and non-wellness office visits with money from your HSA. Wellness visits generally cost you nothing, and several employers have begun to aggressively make additional HSA contributions on your behalf. This can create some short-term cash-flow crunches, but an HSA makes a ton of long-term sense.

HSAs also offer brilliant tax features. The money in an HSA is said to be "triple tax advantaged." This is to suggest that deposits into the account occur pre-tax, the growth in the account is tax-deferred, and the withdrawals for medical purposes are tax-free. Technically, that's better than a 401(k).

When you start an HSA, things can be hairy for the first couple of months, until your HSA balance starts to climb. I recently ran across a company that deposited about $1,300 into employee HSAs after the employees completed certain wellness activities, thus making good health a financial incentive for employees.

Ultimately, though, this is all about being proactive. In your financial life, proactive is budgeting, building an emergency fund, and staying out of debt. That way, when life happens, you are prepared. Does losing your job stink? Absolutely. But having three months' worth of income set aside in your emergency fund helps smooth out the bumps.

As healthcare consumers, we've been trained to be reactive. We pay a bunch of nonrefundable money (premiums), and then we care about our health when something goes wrong.

This is incredibly backwards. HSAs switch up this backward dynamic.

If you're given the option, an HSA paired with a high-deductible health insurance plan should be your choice.

CAR

Everybody wants car insurance protection, but nobody wants to deal with having car insurance. Like most other types of insurance, car insurance can be extremely frustrating because it only pays off when something bad happens. You pray that you never need it; thus, in a way, you're praying that you waste every dollar ever spent on car insurance coverage.

However, there are good financial decisions and bad financial decisions to be had when selecting car insurance coverage. What is the point of having inadequate insurance coverage? Don't be shortsighted. You need to pay attention to this stuff. Some of it saves you money on your premiums. And some of these tips make your life easier if an accident ever were to happen. Following you will find what I find to be the five silliest car insurance mistakes.

▶ **Having too low of a deductible.** If you have an emergency fund that allows you to handle an insurance deductible regardless of whether it's $500 or $1,000, then set your deductible at $1,000. There's no reason to pay the additional premium necessary to secure a low deductible. As you may or may not know, a deductible is the portion of money you are responsible for if you were to file a claim. In other words, if you have a $500 deductible, then you are responsible for the first $500 of costs associated with making you whole. Why waste money on a lower premium when you've got the means to handle an emergency?

▶ **Having no rental car coverage.** If you do get into an accident and lose the use of your car, you may be in trouble. Many people lack free access to another vehicle. So for practicality's sake, having rental car reimbursement coverage on your auto policy can prevent your life from getting crazy-hectic while your car is getting repaired. You don't necessarily need this coverage if you have access to another vehicle or you can seamlessly carpool, but I find that most people should strongly consider rental car reimbursement coverage.

▶ **Having too low of liability limits.** Auto insurance helps you repair your car in the event of an accident. But auto insurance also protects your assets if you were to cause serious damage to someone else. If your liability limits are too low and you are subject to a judgment higher than your limits, then your personal assets can be seized. That's as awful as it sounds.

▶ **Not getting competitive quotes.** Every car insurance company has its own secret recipe of herbs and spices. This is to say that every auto insurance company calculates premiums differently. Some companies put more dependency on your age, gender, driving record, and/or credit score than other companies might. This means there is an auto insurance company that happens to match up with you and your characteristics, and your job is to figure out which company it is. If you choose to have the same insurance company for years on end, just know that you are likely paying way too much for car insurance. This isn't to say you should switch every year, but you should periodically check and see whether you can save money on comparable coverage.

▶ **Filing too many claims.** Look, I know this advice is not what you want to hear, but filing claims can be a really bad idea. Your insurance premium will go up if you file an insurance claim. In fact, if you file too many claims, your insurance company may drop you. I know, I know. What's the point of insurance if you can't use it? You need to think of your car insurance as cata- strophic coverage. Don't file silly little claims that your deductible would absorb anyway. Be smart. This requires restraint, math, and a healthy dose of reality.

Car insurance is a necessary financial tool. Don't be in such a hurry that you neglect to make wise decisions with regard to your coverage choices. It also pays to have a great agent who can explain these concepts to you.

TEEN DRIVERS

If children are part of your world, then you must also under- stand car insurance as it relates to teen drivers. Teens have a reputation for being...um...bad drivers. Don't believe me? Look at the cost to insure them as drivers. Teens speed. Teens wreck. And teens don't make the best driving decisions. You know this for one reason: You were once a teen, too.

Be sure your liability limits on your auto insurance policy reflect the fact that you have a teen driver. In fact, you may want to consider getting additional liability protection through the purchase of an umbrella policy. An umbrella policy pro- vides liability protection above and beyond both your auto and homeowners insurance liability limits. Your assets are at risk if your liability limits are too low. If you were sued and you didn't have enough liability protection, a judgment could result in a financial catastrophe.

RENTERS

Renting is increasingly more common in the United States. According to a study done by Harvard, the renting population in the U.S. grew from 31 percent in 2004 to 35 percent in 2012. Renting is no longer just for a transitional or temporary situation. This natural progression of renting as a more stable lifestyle should lead to insurance, but it has not. The Insurance Information Institute reported that as of 2014, only 37 percent of renters have insurance. This is a big problem. You protect yourself with health and life insurance; it's time you start protecting your stuff.

Your landlord's insurance doesn't cover you. This is the most common myth about renting. You assume your landlord's insurance will cover you. Well, it does cover the house or apartment you are renting, but it doesn't cover your stuff. If your apartment burns down, the apartment will get rebuilt with your landlord's insurance money, but all your stuff will be gone. This is the single most important reason why you need renters insurance.

Additionally, renters insurance is cheap. Unlike other types of insurance, renters insurance is actually extremely affordable. For less than $200 a year, you can insure all your stuff. That's an amazing deal. The thing about insurance—all insurance—is that you hope you don't have to use it. So you may argue it's just throwing away $200 a year, but chances are you throw away more than $200 regularly on junk that doesn't serve nearly as important a role as renters insurance. The small price tag is a more than justified expense.

HOMEOWNERS

You know the old saying: With great homeownership comes great responsibility—or something like that. I think I just lifted and then butchered that saying from a *Spiderman* movie. Your economic risks spike when you become a homeowner. Storms, floods, fires, and even your neighbor slipping and falling on your steps all become your problem when you become a homeowner.

Think of homeowners insurance like renters insurance, except homeowners insurance covers the structure too, as well as liability. While a landlord has to deal with insuring the building in which you live when you're a renter, you have to insure everything when you're a homeowner. You are even financially responsible for events that take place on your property.

If your dog bites someone, or your tree falls on your neighbor's house, or a worker is injured while repairing something in your house, you may be liable for damages. Your homeowners insurance will pay to defend you from any lawsuits and will cover any judgments up to your liability. So, you should take some time to determine the proper amount of liability limits to have on your homeowners insurance policy, based on factors such as your income and lifestyle. You'd be surprised how many insurance companies will refuse you coverage, based on strange factors such as what breed of dog you have.

In most instances, your homeowners insurance premium will be paid through your mortgage company. Your mortgage company usually collects monies, in addition to your principal and interest payments, to pay for your property taxes and homeowners insurance. These additional payments flow into something called an *escrow account*. When your property taxes or insurance invoice is due, the escrow account pays the bill. On a side note, you'll notice that your mortgage payment will increase when your property taxes or homeowners insurance premiums increase.

LIFE

If I were forced to make a list of the different financial products that people generally hate to buy, life insurance would most likely top the list. Because when you purchase life insurance, you're admitting your mortality. And while admitting your mortality is arguably a healthy thing to do, it certainly isn't a fun thing to do.

Life insurance is one of those products that is traditionally thought of as something that only married people or people with children involve themselves in—you know, like minivans. But life insurance can be for single people, too. If you currently have financial dependents, then your family will be without your income when you die. That's a problem. Your life insurance not only replaces your income, but it also funds future financial goals, such as college if you also have children.

But what if you currently don't have dependents? Why do you need life insurance then? Let's examine all the reasons why someone would purchase life insurance regardless of whether they have dependents and see whether the answer exists within these reasons.

▶ **To cover survivor needs.** When you die, your income dies. Your dependents' needs will persist long after you are gone. No dependents generally equals no survivor needs.

▶ **To cover final expenses.** Your family is already upset that you're dead; don't stick them with the funeral bill. A funeral costs between $5,000 and $20,000. You don't really want to force your nondependent family members to pick up that tab in their time of grief.

▶ **To protect future insurability.** Will you always be single? Well, it depends on your dance moves. Just because you're single, that doesn't mean you'll always be single. You may not need life insurance right now, but you might need it in the future. Here's the problem: Although you are currently relatively young and healthy, currently is now over. You are less young and less healthy than you were four seconds ago. What does this mean? It means that technically you are more expensive to insure. And in some cases, your medical issues may prevent you from securing life insurance coverage altogether. You can lock in your health and age by getting life insurance right now. The price of life insurance is based on your age and health. You may not have dependents right now, but you may have them in the future. Buying life insurance now ensures that you will have life insurance once you actually need it. Think of it this way: Do you carry a spare tire in your trunk? Of course you do. You keep it in the trunk just in case you get a flat tire. What I'm trying to say is that marriage is like getting a flat tire. That metaphor fell apart. Never mind.

▶ **To pay off your debts.** If you are the only signer for your debt, then your debts will be paid by your assets upon your death. If you don't have enough assets to offset your debt, then the lender is up a creek. However, if you have a cosigner, then your cosigner is fully responsible for your debt at the time of your death. Yikes. For instance, if your parents cosigned on a loan, then they will owe money on your loan even after you are dead. In some cases parents have been forced to pay back student loans upon their child's death. If you owe money to anyone or you have had anyone cosign on a loan, then please buy enough life insurance to cover your debt.

LIFE INSURANCE WHEN YOU HAVE DEPENDENTS

Life insurance can be challenging for consumers because it deals with two polar opposite concepts: practicality and love. Let's start with the prickly part first, and then we'll tackle the fuzzy stuff.

Practically speaking, when you die, your income dies, too. In fact, if I were forced to disclose the worst aspect of dying, from a financial perspective, I would point to the death of a person's income.

For most people, life insurance should be used to replace the disappearing income. Your lifestyle, your expenses, and your goals are all based on your income. If you die, your income dies, but your survivors' lifestyles, expenses, and goals don't die. A death isn't a blip on the screen that results in quick financial adjustments by the survivors. A death, when not supported by the proper amount of life insurance, rips people from their homes, routines, and dreams.

The proper amount of life insurance will allow your survivors to re-create a vast majority of your net income for quite some time, until they find a new normal. Without a doubt, the most important aspect of life insurance is having the right face amount. Unfortunately and fortunately, I've been there to pick up the financial pieces several times after someone's death. Sadly, hundreds of thousands of dollars don't help much if the situation calls for hundreds of thousands of dollars more.

It's worth noting that there's an old-school approach that primarily relies on life insurance to pay off debts (usually the mortgage). But I've found that this strategy is shortsighted and outdated. While the elimination of a person's largest monthly obligation via a life insurance death benefit is prudent, it can still create major short- and long-term cash flow issues. I like to think of it this way: If you kill the egg-laying chickens, then you will run out of eggs. In other words, if you use a bunch of money that could otherwise be used to create an income, then you lose the ability to create money forever.

Now for love. I told you that life insurance is also about love—although it's a sad day when you start taking love advice from a financial writer. Life insurance is love personified. A person who buys the proper amount of life insurance is securing the future of his or her survivors. Whether the money goes to fund your kids' college education, allow your spouse a chance to grieve without financial stress, or simply provide a lifetime income stream, when you're in a committed relationship, life insurance is part of the deal. It's a way to make good on your commitments, even when you aren't physically around to make good on your commitments.

When I personally contemplate the idea of "peace of mind," I frequently think of life insurance. Peace of mind is often used to justify an insurance purchase. And while I certainly am glad that my car and my house are covered in the event of an insurance event, I'm much more at peace knowing that if I don't come home tomorrow, my family will be financially fine. And that's thanks to life insurance.

LIFE INSURANCE FOR YOUR DEPENDENTS

One of the biggest financial mistakes that I see on a regular basis is the undervaluing of a stay-at-home parent. This is most evident when we look at the life insurance purchased to protect the family. Ignoring the importance of insuring the primary care provider is a heinous error. Especially considering how inexpensive it can be to properly insure a stay-at-home parent.

For example, consider the life of Beth and Paul. Beth is a patent attorney, and Paul stays home with a three-year-old and one-year-old twins. If Paul were to die without life insurance, what would Beth do? How is she supposed to handle the costs for the care of three young children, pay her law school and undergrad student loans, and still make ends meet for monthly bills? The $10,000 of spousal life insurance that her law firm offers her will get Paul buried, and that's about it. Paul likely needs $250,000 to $500,000 worth of life insurance coverage.

Do not neglect to insure the non-breadwinner of a family. Often it can cost less than $30 per month to buy the right life insurance protection.

If any or all of these reasons resonated with you, then you should probably buy life insurance. Consider it a hedge. But how much money should you commit to something that isn't a sure thing? It all depends on your financial situation. If you have dependents and are in a great financial situation, then go ahead and purchase life insurance equal to ten times your income. So if you make $40,000 per year, then purchase life insurance for $400,000. Based on your health, this could cost as little as $25 per month. If you are single and don't have any dependents, you can always make the beneficiary your favorite charity until you switch your beneficiary to your future dependent. Leave a legacy for the organizations that you care about, and then switch the policy to pay the people who will financially suffer in your absence.

If you're single and your financial situation isn't that great, then at least cover your debts. Again, term life insurance isn't that expensive. Term life insurance, as opposed to permanent life insurance, which is sometimes called whole-life or universal life, is temporary coverage. You buy term life insurance usually in blocks of time. For instance, you could buy a $250,000 20-year term policy. The policy would pay your beneficiaries the face amount ($250,000) in the event of your death, as long as your death occurred within the 20-year coverage period.

Permanent coverage provides—you guessed it!—permanent coverage as long as you continue to make premium payments. Most permanent life insurance policies build up a cash component within the policy. It is called *cash value*. Cash value can be borrowed against or withdrawn from the life insurance policy. In some instances, the cash value builds up enough value that you are able to stop making premium payments, and the policy ends up paying for itself. Permanent insurance, by its nature, is much more expensive than term life insurance, but then again it offers several more features.

I don't think it particularly matters what type of life insurance you get, as long as you buy the right amount of coverage. If you need $250,000 of life insurance and all you can afford is term coverage, buy the term coverage. If you need $250,000 of life insurance and all you can afford of the permanent coverage is $50,000, then buy the term coverage.

The most important aspect of life insurance is getting enough coverage for the period you are trying to cover. Your goal should be to become self-insured. That means you don't need life insurance because you have enough permanent income streams and assets to provide for your survivors in the event of your death.

If you're single, you don't have debt, you have enough cash money to cover your funeral expenses, and you have resolved not to have any financial dependents, then you don't need life insurance. Don't buy it.

One strategy you can employ is to take advantage of your life insurance benefits through your employer. I generally prefer that people have life insurance outside of their group coverage because of portability issues (the inability to take the coverage with you to your next job). However, in this instance group coverage is a decent temporary fix to your problem, if you are unsure of what to do.

Make It Easy on Your Survivors

When you die, your passwords die, too. And when you die, the peculiar place you keep your business documents remains peculiar—and unfound. When you die, the financial role that you have held in your family immediately is relinquished.

I recently cleaned up a financial disaster. Money wasn't the issue, yet it was a financial emergency nonetheless. I'm not talking about life insurance and beneficiaries. I'm talking about the transition. How does the surviving spouse re-create the daily financial doings of the person who died?

A widow came to me shortly after her husband passed away for help organizing her financial life. She started the meeting by saying, "He had two different businesses with two different checkbooks, and he has two different credit cards at two different companies. Every phone call that I make in order to make progress creates three new phone calls. He was such a private person that he never wanted me to worry about money. Although he left me plenty of money, I have to unwind his businesses, and I'm so scared."

Money isn't everything. Death begets loss. Loss begets grief. Grief plus disorganization beget anger. It's quite common for people to say things such as "the most loving thing you can do for your surviving spouse is to make sure that you leave adequate life insurance." This is true. But leaving money for someone isn't enough.

The Internet has changed the game when it comes to survivor transitions...and not in a good way. All generations are at risk. Even my wife was at risk. If she didn't know my passwords and know about the intricacies of my business, she would be in financial disarray at the time of my death. Whereas she will have plenty of assets, thanks to life insurance and our savings and investments, she would be quite upset with me for sticking her with my business dealings. They would consume her life while she was trying to raise our children and while she was grieving. This is why we took time to put a transition plan in place.

The problem is worse for our parents. Baby boomers were socialized with traditional gender roles. This means that men primarily dealt with the family finances. The death of a male baby boomer sends shockwaves through his family. The death of a female baby boomer is equally awful, but the financial transition isn't as severe based on how 1950s gender roles were established. This is a real problem. Your parents and your grandparents may have financial plans for their death, but it's unlikely that they have transition plans in place. And it's unlikely that you have a transition plan in place at all.

Here are the things you need to consider to help make the worst moment in your loved one's life a little easier.

- **Have a password plan.** I use a password vault program, such as LastPass. I have one password to remember. The rest of the passwords are managed by "the vault." My wife just needs to know one password, and she can open the vault to all my other passwords. It's secure, and it's the best way for your loved one to access your important information.

- **Discuss your job.** Your significant other needs to know important details about your business/job. He or she needs to know where you bank, where your retirement accounts are, and many other mysterious details. Your spouse also needs to have an awareness of your business advisors, your lawyer, your accountant, and any financial advisors.

■ **Lift the curtain.** Do you have weird financial habits? Yeah, me too. Please, please, *please* let your partner know what is going on. Regular budget meetings help with this. Regular discussions about your financial life will address this.

■ **Ask up.** Ask your parents what their plan is. Don't get this twisted. You aren't asking about their finances; you're asking about their transition plan. It's a loving conversation: "Dad, where do you bank? Who's your lawyer? What do I need to know in order to take care of mom when you die?"

■ **Ask down.** Ask your adult children what their plan is. It's show and tell. You show them your plan and then ask to see their plan. Discuss the importance of a healthy transition plan.

Your significant other's right to grieve peacefully is important. Allow him or her to do this. Once again, to be clear, this has nothing to do with money. It's all about organization.

DISABILITY

You might have noticed how frequently people talk about and think about life insurance. They should. The death of a loved one leaves many craters, with financial craters being among the most significant. Yet no one is really talking about disability insurance. Unfortunately, many financial plans lack disability insurance. If you become disabled without having adequate disability insurance in place, then your financial life will crumble.

Several years ago, my father's best friend was stricken with a horrific medical condition. As you can imagine, this medical condition wasn't in the man's life plans. He was at the height of his career, and he had four growing children and a loving wife. He was a smart guy with plenty of income and a bright financial future, as long as he was able to continue to earn his bountiful income. His medical condition had other plans. He was unable to earn his income.

Fortunately, yet not surprisingly, my father's friend was prepared. He had great disability insurance. No, not just the disability insurance that many of us have through our employers; he also had supplemental disability coverage. He had the type of supplemental coverage that a person buys when he understands that a 35-year-old man is three-and-a-half times more likely to become disabled than to die.

Insurance, as you know, is a numbers game. Men and women much smarter than you and me crunch numbers, study risks, and understand trends. If they think we are more likely to be disabled than to die, shouldn't we take them seriously? Shouldn't we protect ourselves from financial tragedies that are more likely than death itself?

If your employer offers you disability insurance, they'll most likely offer you one of two types coverage—or both. The first type of disability insurance coverage is short-term disability insurance. It usually kicks in within 30 days of a person becoming disabled (temporarily or permanently), and it typically covers the individual for up to 26 weeks. The policy will cover somewhere between 50 and 66 percent of your income, which will still be taxed.

Next, if your employer provides you with long-term disability (LTD) insurance, your LTD will pick up where your short-term disability left off. The coverage amount is almost always similar to the short-term disability coverage—somewhere between 50 and 66 percent of your income. If your employer purchased the coverage for you with pre-tax dollars, your disability income will be subject to income tax. If *you* paid for your coverage, either through your employer or on your own with after-tax dollars, you will receive your disability income tax-free. LTD benefits can last any number of years. Five to 10 years' worth of benefits is common, but some policies provide disability income through age 67.

Ask yourself this serious question: Could you and your family survive on 50 to 66 percent of your income for a long period of time? Me neither. Did I mention that the 50 to 66 percent of your income is likely to be taxed? Fortunately, you may be able to purchase supplemental disability coverage on your own. Supplemental coverage is usually purchased with after-tax money; thus, you receive the benefits tax-free. You can sometimes purchase supplemental coverage through your employer, but it's also commonly purchased through insurance agents and financial planners.

The terms of your coverage are also very important. Some disability insurance is classified as *own occupation*—or *own occ*, as industry people call it. Own occ means you are technically disabled if you cannot do your specific job. *Any occupation* coverage—or *any occ*—specifies that a person isn't technically disabled until he or she is unable to perform *any* occupation. As you can imagine, there's a giant difference between own occ and any occ. These differences account for a major cost discrepancy between own occ and any occ. Because a person is considered disabled when he or she can't perform his or her specific job, own occ coverage is much more desirable and justifiably more expensive.

Disability benefits are available through the Social Security Administration as well, but sadly, the analysis of Social Security Disability Insurance (SSDI) benefits often meander into a discussion about how to get classified as disabled—right, wrong, or indifferent. This is why I encourage you to focus on what you can proactively do to protect yourself, your family, and your income.

Take time to understand what's offered to you through your employer, and explore supplemental coverage options with your insurance agent or financial planner.

REVIEW YOUR COVERAGE ANNUALLY

You obviously don't want to spend a great deal of time obsessing over what could go wrong with your life, but it certainly is prudent to reexamine your insurance needs annually. If you have enough insurance needs, it makes sense to find a trusted insurance agent. Their expertise can mean the difference between spending money on coverage that helps you and wasting money on inadequate coverage.

CHAPTER 9

THE PLAN

Something became abundantly clear upon writing books about every decade of a person's financial life. Your forties make up the hardest decade of all. To be honest, this surprised me. Each decade of a person's life presents challenges, but there's something ominous about your forties. No, not the "over the hill" jokes and the instances of midlife crises. After considering every age from 20 to 70, I've realized that the years in your forties can be downright brutal.

Prepare yourself for a little bit of dramatic writing. If you leave your forties with significant financial struggles, there is very little recourse for your future.

If you hit 50 and you are still mired in overspending, debt, and an empty retirement account, you're in serious trouble. The same couldn't be said when you hit 30 or 40. And as if this pressure weren't intense enough, go ahead and throw in the possibility of trying to fund college for your children. And by the way, if you make the wrong choices in funding their education, you'll exit your forties with even more debt in the form of Parent PLUS Loans.

To be transparent, no other book I've ever written has been as direct and as slightly terrifying as the last two paragraphs have been. But when I think back on the tens of thousands of financial lives that I've dug through in the last decade and a half, I'm sad to report that the most helpless situations are present in 49- and 50-year-olds.

With every passing year, the convenient excuses as to why you aren't where you want to be financially seem to disappear. The excuses stop feeling convenient and begin to ring of apathy. At what point is your inaction benign? And at what point is your inaction a dereliction of duty to yourself? Awareness without action is a bad place to be. You must take action.

For every day that you don't address your debt, your debt gets worse. For every day that you don't fund an emergency fund, the greater the impact of small financial emergencies will be. And for every day that you don't save for retirement, the harder saving will become for your future self.

You need a plan. More specifically, you need a plan that takes into account what you've done and what you haven't done. I've found that people often get paralyzed when flooded with the tasks they haven't completed. Creating a plan for your finances sounds much more intimidating than it actually is. Figuring out what to do next needs to be a very simple process. There's only one way to achieve planning simplicity. We're going to harken back to yesteryear and employ the most reader-driven writing technique of all time: the *Choose Your Own Adventure* book.

If you aren't familiar with *Choose Your Own Adventure* books, you're in for a treat. Navigate through the following series of questions. As you answer the questions, jump to the section that applies to your answer. Follow the directions, make choices, follow more directions, and before you know it, you've taken action.

Do not overcomplicate this process. Your focus and action should be singular. Don't just start throwing money at all of your different financial priorities. If everything is a priority, then nothing is a priority. It's easy to get stressed out when you feel the pressure to get so much accomplished all at the same time.

CHOOSE YOUR OWN ADVENTURE

Do not skip ahead. Answer each question and then follow the plan provided.

QUESTIONS

A. Have you started contributing enough to maximize the match offered by your employer-sponsored retirement plan—for example, your 401(k)?

If yes, go to Question B.

If no, go to Plan 1.

B. Do you maintain a budget on a monthly basis?

If yes, go to Question C.

If no, go to Plan 2.

C. Do you have $1,000 in savings?

If yes, go to Question D.

If no, go to Plan 3.

D. Do you have the proper insurances discussed in Chapter 8?

If yes, go to Question E.

If no, go to Plan 4.

E. Do you have any credit card debt?

If yes, go to Plan 5.

If no, go to Question F.

F. Do you have a fully funded emergency fund (three months of expenses)?

> If yes, go to question G.

> If no, go to Plan 6.

G. Do you have children?

> If yes, go to Question H.

> If no, go to Question J.

H. Have you established a sincere college funding strategy for your kids?

> If yes, go to Question I.

> If no, go to Plan 7.

I. Are you making consistent deposits into a college fund for your children?

> If yes, go to Question J.

> If no, go to Plan 8.

J. Do you have student loan debt?

> If yes, go to Plan 9.

> If no, go to Question K.

K. Do you plan on increasing the percentage of your income you put toward your retirement plan every year?

> If yes, go to Question L.

> If no, go to Plan 10.

L. Do you have a financial advisor?

> If yes, go to Question M.

> If no, go to Plan 11.

M. Are you maxing out your retirement plans?

> If yes, go to Question N.

> If no, go to Plan 12.

N. Are you saving at least 20 percent of your take-home pay?

> If yes, go to Plan 13.

> If no, also go to Plan 13.

O. Have you paid off your home?

> If yes, excellent work.

> If no, go to Plan 14.

PLANS

1. Do it. Talk to your human resources person and ask them the process. You may have to wait for open-enrollment season, or you may be able to fill out the proper paperwork and get started today. Once you've set it up and your first contribution takes place, proceed to Question B.

2. Your focus must instantly turn to resourcefulness. While earning more money may be a solution to some of your financial issues, taking control of your spending will allow you to become efficient and purposeful. Fill out your budget chart and start cutting spending so

you can put a focused amount of money toward your goals on a monthly basis. Once you've captured some money to put toward your goals, proceed to Question C.

3. Saving $1,000 now becomes your primary focus. In fact, you should obsess over it. Work extra hours if possible. Reduce your spending. Your $1,000 starter emergency fund will allow you to address other areas of your financial life without leaving you too vulnerable to life's surprises. Once you've saved $1,000, proceed to Question D.

4. Your decision to address your financial priorities is a noble one, but you risk everything if you don't account for risk. Insuring yourself properly—whether we're talking life insurance, car insurance, renters insurance, or homeowners insurance—isn't necessarily expensive, and it can prevent your financial life from blowing up. Once you've properly addressed your insurance needs, proceed to Question E.

5. Using the momentum method you learned in Chapter 2, create your debt pay-down table and start working it. Eliminate the smallest debt first and keep grinding until your debts are paid off. When people decide to address their debt, it's not uncommon for them to feel like the money that flows toward debt reduction is spent money. Because if the money doesn't go toward fun stuff and the money isn't being saved, then it must be considered spent, right? Well, that's simply not true. Paying off debt has the exact same effect on a person's net worth as saving money does. Once your credit card debts are vanquished, proceed to Question F.

6. A fully funded emergency fund is the closest thing you can be to bulletproof. Your focus can officially turn to wiping out your other debts, saving for a major purchase, and investing for retirement. Once your emergency fund is fully funded, proceed to Question G.

7. You owe it to your children to take the time to decide how their college education will be paid for if they choose to go to college. If you don't take the time to put thought into this decision, the result can be a nasty mix of debt, regret, and a delay in retirement. You cannot just hope that things work out. They won't. If you plan on participating in your child's education expenses, start saving money today. If you need to clean up some debt, that's fine, but just know that the income you've put toward your debt should be reallocated to college saving once the debts are paid off. Proceed to Question I.

8. Begin by exploring the 529 plan offered through your state of residence. If your state's plan offers tax incentives, strongly consider using your state's plan. Proceed to Question J.

9. Turn up the pressure on yourself to pay down your student loans. Sure, they can hang out in your life for a few more years, but if you've already accomplished all of the other questions and plans before this one, then it's time to be done with student loans. Focus all the money you freed up for your financial priorities on paying off your student loans. When you've accomplished this, proceed to Question K.

10. Your goal should be to save a higher percentage of your income every year until you retire. If you do this, you will easily be able to transition from your work income to your retirement income. Not only will you have enough money set aside for the future, but you also will be much less dependent on money altogether. Proceed to Question L.

11. A good financial advisor can enhance your financial future. Given that you've made it to this point in your adventure, you will have eliminated your financial past, mastered your financial present, and turned your sights to your financial future. Your financial future is exactly what a good financial advisor specializes in. Set a deadline to interview two or three financial advisors in the next 30 days. Let them know you've cleaned up your debt, have solid spending habits, and are primarily looking for someone to help you harness your income to fund your future. Proceed to Question M.

12. The IRS will actually cut you a break if you let them. By IRS code, you can deduct a significant amount of money from your income if you deposit that money into a qualified retirement fund. Stay current on contribution limits, as they change nearly every year. As you've learned, when you go without that income now, you begin to break your dependency on your work income, which will serve you well in retirement. Proceed to Question N.

13. Do you want to get "in the zone"? Then don't create new financial obligations by taking on debts and new payments. It's not enough to have a significant amount of discretionary income with no true obligations. You must consistently transition this freedom into savings. If you are consistently blowing through your discretionary income, then you are dependent on the income. Once you've begun to save 20 percent of your take-home pay toward nonqualified investments, push yourself further. And now on to Question O.

14. You can take the pressure off of your retirement income by paying off your home as quickly as possible. Once your home is paid off, you will be able to save more money, invest more money, and most importantly, reduce the amount of retirement income you will need to cover your expenses.

EXTREME SOLUTIONS

As I mentioned at the beginning of this chapter, your forties are a make-it-or-break-it decade. You are either on track or off track. If you are off track and you have no reasonable justification for thinking you'll be back on track soon, you must take extreme measures. If you aren't on track as you leave your forties, I can't just stand by and say good luck. I've got to give you a plan, too. But your plan is intense and extreme.

There are two major extreme solutions that I've seen work. Are they fun? Absolutely not. Do they ultimately relieve a plethora of financial stress and get people back on track? Absolutely. The first solution: Get an additional job.

GET AN ADDITIONAL JOB

There are two solutions to any cash flow problem: spend less money or make more money. That's it. It makes sense, though, because those are the two elements of cash flow. Logic dictates that if you adjust one of the two variables of any equation, change will occur. In this instance, though, it's been my experience that most people believe more money is the solution to their problems, rather than less spending. In fact, I'd go as far as to say 90 percent of people point to more income as their solution. Take that with a grain of salt, though. We all know that 65 percent of statistics are made up, and the other 55 percent are inaccurate.

More income can be a solution once you've exhausted your opportunities to decrease your spending. But increasing your income isn't easy; it's an extreme activity. And that's why it's an extreme solution.

You're going to need a bigger net—net positive cash flow, that is. And once you can't cut expenses anymore, then more income is the solution. But there's a giant *but*. If you add more income without addressing your propensity to waste, you will make your problem worse. If you add more financial resources (money) to a situation that isn't resourceful, then this whole plan will backfire.

Dumping more money into a financial boat full of holes is a bad idea. You might actually have done this before. If you've ever gotten a raise and not really seen the positive economic impact on your life, then you know what I'm talking about. And by positive economic impact, I don't mean fun. Fun is fun, but fun isn't keeping a keen eye on your future.

You shouldn't bother starting the second-job search process until you know how much money you need to make. If you don't know why you are working a second job, then why get a second job? The *why* happens when you know exactly how much money you need to make. Would an extra $500 per month improve your financial future? Cool. Find a job that can accomplish that. Your second job is mercenary money. You are working to accomplish something specific. Don't just throw the extra money into the pot with the rest of your money that isn't making ends meet.

You also need to determine how long you should work a second job. A second job is easier to swallow when there's an end game. You should also know that getting a second job isn't embarrassing. In fact, it's awesome! You are stepping up and taking control of your financial life. Not only is it not embarrassing, but I'd tell everyone I knew about your commitment to your family and your future. Financial problems rarely solve themselves. Don't stand by and hope that you are the exception to the rule. Take action.

SELL YOUR HOUSE

Think through all the things in your life that could cause financial stress. What you will notice is that these things are limited to just a few major categories: house, debt, job, and family. The reason for this is simple: a perceived permanency. In all four of those categories, there isn't an easy and convenient end game. Want a new job? You'll have to quit your current one and find a new one. That's long and hard. Want to stop the stress that comes with money and family? You'll need months of work or a very ugly separation. You get the point. Financial stress hits us the hardest when we feel like the solution is too extreme for our liking. But is it?

In the case of housing, the solution seems painful, but it's the most peace-producing solution around. But first, let's briefly examine how housing has the ability to dominate you. Without question, housing is an American's number-one expense. Whereas financial experts prefer that you limit your exposure to housing costs to 25 percent of your net income, many Americans push the limits way beyond this. I consider anyone who dedicates more than 40 percent of net pay to housing to be clinically overhoused.

Overhousing is an awful, awful thing. Two awfuls? Yes, two awfuls. Why? Because only two things can solve the over-housing problem: a significant increase in income or moving. I've found that people are more likely to hold out hope for an extreme raise than they are to move. This is a big problem. Overhousing is sneaky stressful. When you commit more than

40 percent of your household income to housing, you only leave 60 percent of your income for all of your other expenses. And this usually means the first cuts to happen affect savings and charity. Anecdotally, it's been my experience that anyone dealing with overhousing is also dealing with significant consumer debt.

Several phenomena cause overhousing, including overreaching, decreased income, and very low (just above poverty level) income. And as mentioned before, only two things solve overhousing: a significant increase in income or changing housing. When you're renting, changing your housing is in play and is a more common technique than for those who are over-housed in a mortgage. Why don't people who are figuratively killing themselves with an objectively unaffordable mortgage fix their situation? Lots of reasons.

Your home is not only your largest expense, but it's often your largest emotional anchor. The thought of something as seemingly trivial as money getting in the way of something as seemingly meaningful as your family home is vomit-inducing. We'll fight and scrap to keep the threads that hold us together intact, but we don't realize that the threads that are currently pulling apart are the bigger issue.

This is an extreme solution. It's not easy, but it can be a lifesaver. If you have equity in your house, then the equity may be able to repair some of the other damage that exists in your world. If you have no equity in your house, then the extreme reduction in housing expenses is still reason for a change.

Consider this overly simplified example. If your net household income is $4,000 per month and your mortgage is $1,600 or more, than taking your housing expenses back to the proper level will reduce your housing expense to $1,000. "But it's just $600," you say. Yes. It's $600 you *don't* have the luxury of throwing around on something you can't afford. That's the point. You would need a 60 percent pay increase to truly be able to afford your mortgage ($6,400 × 25% = $1,600).

If you're overhoused and you aren't experiencing financial awfulness, then move along. There's nothing for you to see here. I guess we should take a brief moment to explore signs of financial awfulness. If you have copious amounts of consumer debt, if you are late on your mortgage payment, if you've had to dip into your savings to pay your regular bills, or if you haven't regularly saved money on a monthly basis over the last 12 months, then you might be in trouble.

If I hit your nail on the head, you're currently not feeling too good about this. That's okay; discomfort can be good. We've no doubt identified a major problem. You don't have to sell your house, but I'm suggesting it might be the best solution. At the very least, admit to the problem and then find a better solution. A 60 percent pay increase is a pretty solid solution. Just remind me, where do you get one of those?

YOUR DILIGENCE AND DISCIPLINE WILL PAY DIVIDENDS

I'm not asking that you spend hours per month dealing with your financial life. In fact, I'm asking that you dedicate around 30 minutes per month to make sure you don't have to spend hours per month worrying about your financial life. Every month you should run through your budget, check on your debt-repayment schedule, and then reconfirm your current singular objective.

You will be faced with the temptations of convenience, apathy, and ignorance. But none of those things will give you the sort of financial life you really want.

Don't ignore your financial past. Be wise in the present. And prepare for your future. It's *Your Money Life*.

INDEX

Numerics

15-year mortgages, 109–112
30-year mortgages, 109–112
401(k) loans, 30–31
401(k) plan, 174–175
529 College Savings Plan, 175–176
2009 Credit Card Reform Act, 23

A

abundance spending, 52
agents, insurance, 207
air leaks, reducing spending, 69
amounts owed, credit score factors, 149
AnnualCreditReport website, 138
annuities, 176–178
assets, 159–160
attitude toward debt, 7

B

Balances section (credit report), 140
bank credit cards
2009 Credit Card Reform Act, 23
and debt, 21–23
Federal Reserve data analysis on, 23
Fidelity study of, 23
Good Debt/Bad Debt rating, 23–24
increased usage, 22–23

bankruptcy filings, 27
bonds, 170
broker checks, 195
budgets
activities and processes, 78–79
for big-box store shopping, 97–98
children's expenses, 96
comparing spending to expenses, 99
debt reduction, 95
education, 94
financial independence, 76
fixed income and expenses, 77–78
forties as most financially challenging time of your life, 8–9
ideal household
based on take home pay, 82
charitable organization, 89–90
clothing, 90
entertainment, 91
groceries and dining out, 85–87
holidays and gifts, 92
importance of, 80–82
medical expenses, 91
miscellaneous expenses, 92
rent/mortgage, 82–83
savings, 87–88
transportation, 83–84
utilities, 88–89

importance of, 76
income independence, 76–77
reasons for, 79–80
student loans, 93
vacation, 95–96
what this book will teach you, 8–9
buying *versus* leasing car, 121–124

C

cable channels, reducing spending, 72
cars
    ideal household budget, 83–84
    insurance, 210–213
    leasing *versus* buying, 121–124
    loans
        and debt, 25–26
        Experian Automotive data, 25
        Good Debt/Bad Debt rating, 26
    major purchases, 119–127
    pre-funding, 124–125
    preowned, 125
cash flow, 50, 52
cash value, 220–221
cell phones, reducing spending, 69, 72
charitable organization, ideal household budget, 89–90
cheap-money fallacy, 15–16

children
    budgeting expenses, 96
    establishing credit, 150–154
    and financial complexity, 4
    financially grounded, 4
    teen driver insurance, 212–213
claims, car insurance, 212
Closed Accounts section (credit report), 139
clothing budget, 90
coffee drinks, reducing spending, 72
collection debt, 33–34
college
    529 College Savings Plan, 175–176
    EFC (Expected Family Contribution), 131
    FAFSA (Free Application For Student Aid), 127–128
    FinAid chart, 128–129
    financial aid, 130–131
    major purchases, 127–132
    price inflation, 128–129
    saving for, 187–188
commission-based financial advisors, 192, 194
commitment, debt pay-down, 38, 46–47
common stock, 169
confidence, consumer, 47
consumer confidence, 47
consumer-driven healthcare, 208

cosigners, 151–152
credit
    children's, 150–154
    forties as most financially
        challenging time of
        your life, 9
    importance of good,
        136–137
    improving bad, 146–148
    maintaining good, 146–148
    qualifying for, 132
    running debit as, 62
    what this book will teach
        you, 9
credit cards
    bank, 22–24
    cash back rewards, 57
    "charge everything and pay it
        off at end of month"
        method, 53–58
    secured, 154
    store, 24–25
credit history, credit score
    factors, 149
credit reports
    AnnualCreditReport
        website, 138
    components of, 139–140
    disputable items, 146–147
    Equifax credit bureau, 147
    Experian credit bureau, 147
    inaccuracies, 146–147
    ordering, 138
    periodically checking, 141
    TransUnion credit bureau,
        147

credit scores
    amounts owed factors, 149
    calculation, 148–150
    credit history factors, 149
    financial paradox, 135
    importance of good credit,
        136–137
    inquiries, new credit factors,
        149–150
    measurement, 134
    payment history factor,
        148–149
    point of reference, 143–144
    range, 143
    repairing and building,
        141–144
    rise or fall in, 145
    types of credit in use factors,
        150

D

death
    life insurance, 215–221
    making it easier on survivors,
        222–224
debit cards
    fees associated with, 60
    misusing, 59–60
    selecting debit or credit
        when using, 61–62
    spending with, 58–61

debt. *See also* Good Debt/Bad Debt ratings
attitude toward, 7
blame for, 36–37
cheap-money fallacy, 15–16
growth in debt levels, 14
paying down
blame for debt, 36
building momentum with small debt victories, 43, 46
challenges, 38
commitment toward, 38, 46–47
debt elimination process, 42–47
debt reduction budget, 95
financial stress, 37
mapping out debt, 43–45
math method, 39–40
momentum method, 41
shotgun method, 41–42
staying out of debt after, 48
relationship with, 37
shift in perspective toward, 47
staying out of, 48

types
401(k) loans, 30–31
bank credit cards, 22–24
car loans, 25–26
collection debt, 33–34
home loans, 26–27
judgments, 34–35
lines of credit (secured and unsecured), 28–29
medical, 27–28
parent student loans, 20–22
personal loans (from family or friends), 32
personal loans (from financial institution), 31–32
store credit cards, 24–25
student loans, 18–20
tax, 33
what this book will teach you, 7
deductible, car insurance, 210
Delinquent section (credit report), 139
dependents, life insurance, 217–221
Derogatory section (credit report), 139
dining out
ideal household budget, 85–87
reducing spending, 66

disability insurance, 225–227
Dividend Reinvestment
    Programs (DRIPs), 169
dividends, 169
Dow Jones, 171–172
DRIPs (Dividend Reinvestment
    Programs), 169

E

education
    budgets, 94
    college
        529 College Savings Plan,
            175–176
        EFC (Expected Family
            Contribution), 131
        FAFSA (Free Application
            For Student Aid),
            127–128
        FinAid chart, 128–129
        financial aid, 130–131
        major purchases, 127–132
        price inflation, 128–129
        saving for, 187–188
    student loans
        budgets, 93
        debt, 18–20
        federal (subsidized), 19
        Good Debt/Bad Debt
            rating, 19
        parent, 20–22
        Pell Grants, 21
        Perkins Loans, 21
        private, 20

EFC (Expected Family
    Contribution) form, 21,
    131
employer match, retirement
    plan, 165, 181–187
entertainment budgets, 91
Equifax credit bureau, 147
equity line of credit, 29
escrow accounts, 215
ETFs (Exchange Traded
    Funds), 171
Exchange Traded Funds
    (ETFs), 171
Expected Family Contribution
    (EFC) form, 21, 131
Experian Automotive car loan
    data, 25
Experian credit bureau, 147

F

FAFSA (Free Application For
    Student Aid), 21,
    127–128
family or friends, personal
    loans from, 32
Federal Reserve data analysis,
    23
federal (subsidized) student
    loans, 19
fee-based financial advisors,
    194–195
fee-only financial advisors, 192,
    194–195
Fidelity study, 23
fiduciary responsibility, 194

financial advisors
abilities to teach, 191
attentiveness, 191
broker checks, 195
commission-based, 192, 194
evaluating, 195–200
fee-based, 194–195
fee-only, 192, 194–195
fees, 193–195
hiring, 188–203
knowledge levels, 190
performance in relation to income used toward financial goals, 199
performance in relation to index, 196–199
risk radars, 191–192
risk tolerance determination, 200–203
titles associated with, 189
financial aid, college, 130–131
financial independence, 76, 182–183
financial plan
additional jobs, 239–240
diligence and discipline, 244
extreme solutions, 238–243
importance of, 230–231
questions, 232–238
selling your house, 241–243
what this book will teach you, 11
fixed annuities, 177
fixed bills, utility bills, 67
food
ideal household budget, 85–87
reducing spending, 64–66

Free Application For Student Aid (FAFSA), 21, 127–128
friends, personal loans from, 32
funds
Exchange Traded Funds, 171
index, 172
mutual, 170–171
target-date, 172–174

G

gifts, ideal household budget, 92
glide path, 172
Good Debt/Bad Debt ratings. *See also* debt
401(k) loans, 31
bank credit cards, 23–24
car loans, 26
collection debt, 34
home loans, 27
judgments, 35
lines of credit, 29
medical bills, 28
parent student loans, 22
personal loans (from family or friends), 32
personal loans (from financial institution), 32
scales, 17–18
store credit cards, 25
student loans, 19
tax debt, 33

groceries
  ideal household budget,
    85–87
  reducing spending, 64–65

H

hard inquiry, 140
health insurance, 208–210
Health Savings Account
  (HSA), 27, 208–209
HELOC (home equity line of
  credit), 29, 114–115
holidays, ideal household
  budget, 92
home improvements, 114–119
home loans (mortgage). *See
  also* housing purchase
  and debt, 26–27
  Good Debt/Bad Debt rating,
    27
  ideal household budget,
    82–83
homeowners insurance,
  214–215
house, selling, 241–243
household budget. *See* ideal
  household budget
housing purchase, 102. *See
  also* home loans
  (mortgage)
  15-year *versus* 30-year
    mortgages, 109–112
  benchmark numbers for,
    104–105

emotional entity, 103
home improvements,
  114–119
housing liquidity, 105–106
importance of hiring good
  realtors, 112–114
monthly commitment,
  103–105
mortgage repayment
  summary, 109–112
owning too much home,
  105–109
renting *versus* buying,
  108–109
HSA (Health Savings
  Account), 27, 208–209

I

ideal household budget
  based on take-home pay, 82
  charitable organization,
    89–90
  clothing, 90
  entertainment, 91
  groceries and dining out,
    85–87
  holidays and gifts, 92
  importance of, 80–82
  medical expenses, 91
  miscellaneous expenses, 92
  rent, 82–83
  savings, 87–88
  transportation, 83–84
  utilities, 88–89

income independence, 76–77
index, 171
index annuities, 177
index funds, 172
inflation-adjusted retirement
    income, 185
inquiries, credit score factors,
    149–150
Inquiries section (credit
    report), 140
insurance
    agents, 207
    annual reviews, 228
    car, 210–213
    disability, 225–227
    health, 208–210
    homeowners, 214–215
    importance of, 207
    life, 215–221
    renters, 213–214
    what this book will teach
        you, 10
interest-free grace periods,
    store credit cards, 24
Internet service, reducing
    spending, 71
investing
    employer match, 181–187
    investment types
        401(k), 175
        529 College Savings Plan,
            175–176
        annuities, 176–178
        bonds, 170
        ETFs (Exchange Traded
            Funds), 171

index funds, 172
IRA (Individual
    Retirement
    Account), 174
mutual funds, 170–171
Roth IRA, 174
stock, 169
target-date funds,
    172–174
reasons for not waiting,
    179–181
versus saving, 158
terms, 168
what this book will teach
    you, 10
IRA (Individual Retirement
    Account), 174

J

judgments
    and debt, 34–35
    Good Debt/Bad Debt rating,
        35
    levies, 35
    liens, 35
    wage garnishment, 34
junk bonds, 170

L

landline phones, reducing
    spending, 69
leasing cars, 121–124
levies, 35
liability limits, car insurance,
    211

liens, 35
life insurance
for dependents, 219–221
reasons for, 215–217
when you have dependents,
217–219
light bills, 68
lines of credit
and debt, 28–29
Good Debt/Bad Debt rating,
29
secured and unsecured,
28–29
loan declination, 152–153
loans
401(k)
and debt, 30–31
Good Debt/Bad Debt
rating, 31
car
and debt, 25–26
Experian Automotive
data, 25
Good Debt/Bad Debt
rating, 26
home (mortgage)
and debt, 26–27
Good Debt/Bad Debt
rating, 27
ideal household budget,
82–83
personal
from family or friends, 32
from financial institution,
31–32

student
budgets, 93
debt, 18–20
federal (subsidized), 19
Good Debt/Bad Debt
rating, 19
parent, 20–22
Pell Grants, 21
Perkins Loans, 21
private, 20
long-term disability (LTD)
insurance, 226
long-term savings, 164–165
loyalty programs, store credit
cards, 24
LTD (long-term disability)
insurance, 226

M

major purchases. *See also*
spending
benchmark numbers for,
104–105
cars, 119–127
college, 127–132
forties as most financially
challenging time of
your life, 9
housing purchase, 102
15-year *versus* 30-year
mortgages, 109–112
emotional entity, 103
home improvements,
114–119
housing liquidity,
105–106

importance of hiring good realtors, 112–114

monthly commitment, 103–105

mortgage repayment summary, 109–112

owning too much home, 105–109

renting *versus* buying, 108–109

qualifying for credit, 132

what this book will teach you, 9

manual underwriting, 155

MasterCard, 22

math method (debt pay-down process), 39–40

medical bills

bankruptcy filings, 27

and debt, 27–28

Good Debt/Bad Debt rating, 28

HSA (Health Savings Account), 27

ideal household budget, 91

NerdWallet Health study, 27

mid-term savings, 167–168

miscellaneous expenses, ideal household budget, 92

Mock Retirement, 185

momentum method (debt pay-down process), 41

money

cheap-money fallacy, 15–16

keeping too much available, 50–51

nonqualified, 167

mortgages. *See* home loans

mutual funds, 170–171

N

negative equity, 120

NerdWallet Health study, 27

net cash flow, 50

net worth

calculation, 159

as indicator of financial health, 23

as wealth-building tool, 159–163

nonqualified money, 167

O

Open Accounts section (credit report), 139

own occupation disability insurance, 227

P

Parent PLUS Loans, 21–22, 188

parent student loans, 20–22

parents of fortysomethings, involvement in financial lives, 4–6

password plan, 223
past debt. *See* debt
paying down debt
  blame for debt, 36
  building momentum with
    small debt victories, 43,
    46
  challenges, 38
  commitment toward, 38,
    46–47
  debt elimination process,
    42–47
  debt reduction budget, 95
  financial stress, 37
  mapping out debt, 43–45
  math method, 39–40
  momentum method, 41
  shotgun method, 41–42
  staying out of debt after, 48
payment history, credit score
  factors, 148–149
Payments section (credit
  report), 140
Pell Grants, 21
pension, 164
Perkin Loans, 21
permanent life insurance, 220
personal loans
  from family or friends, 32
  from financial institution,
    31–32
phones, reducing spending, 69,
  72

plan, financial
  additional jobs, 239–240
  diligence and discipline, 244
  extreme solutions, 238–243
  importance of, 230–231
  questions, 232–238
  selling your house, 241–243
  what this book will teach
    you, 11
Ponzi schemes, 192
possessions. *See* major
  purchases
preferred stock, 169
pre-owned cars, 125
private student loans, 20
Public Records section (credit
  report), 140
purchases. *See* major
  purchases; spending

R
realtors, 112–114
reducing spending, 63–73
rent
  ideal household budget,
    82–83
  renters insurance, 213–214
  renting *versus* buying home,
    108–109
rental car coverage, 211
restaurants, dining out
  ideal household budget,
    85–87
  reducing spending, 66

retirement
   60 percent stock and 40
      percent bond asset mix,
      185–186
   401(k) loans, 30–31
   401(k) plan, 175
   employer match, 165,
      181–187
   inflation-adjusted income,
      185
   IRA (Individual Retirement
      Account), 174
   Roth IRA, 174
   savings calculator, 183–184
risk tolerance, 200–203
Roth IRA, 174

S

saving
   for college, 187–188
   ideal household budget,
      87–88
   versus investing, 158
   long-term, 164–165
   mid-term, 167–168
   purpose of, 158
   role of net worth as wealth-
      building tool, 159–163
   short-term, 165–166
   what this book will teach
      you, 10
scarcity, 54–55
second jobs, 239–240
secured credit cards, 154

secured lines of credit, 28–29
selling your house, 241–243
shortage, 50
short-term disability insurance,
   226
short-term savings, 165–166
shotgun method (debt pay-
   down process), 41–42
Simplicity-Needs Paradox,
   70–73
Small Business Job Protection
   Act of 1996, 175
Social Security, 164
Social Security Disability
   Insurance (SSDI), 227
soft inquiry, 140
S&P 500 (Standard & Poor's
   500), 171
spending. *See also* major
   purchases
   abundance, 52
   budgeting for, 99
   cash flow management, 50,
      52
   categories
      dining out, 66
      groceries, 64–65
      list of, 63
      new necessities, 70–73
      utilities, 67–70
   "charge everything and pay it
      off at end of month"
      method, 53–58
   with debit card, 58–61
   feeling of financial comfort,
      52

forties as most financially
  challenging time of
  your life, 8
how credit card complicates,
  53–58
keeping too much money
  available, 50–51
reducing, 63–73
selecting debit or credit
  when using debit cards,
  61–62
splurging, 73–74
with tracking, 50
what this book will teach
  you, 8
splurging, 73–74
SSDI (Social Security
  Disability Insurance), 227
stock, 169
store credit cards
and debt, 24–25
Good Debt/Bad Debt rating,
  25
interest-free grace periods,
  24
loyalty programs, 24
student loans
budgets, 93
debt, 18–20
federal (subsidized), 19
Good Debt/Bad Debt rating,
  19
parent, 20–22
Pell Grants, 21
Perkins Loans, 21
private, 20

subsidized (federal) student
  loans, 19
supplemental insurance, 226
surplus, 50

T
target-date funds, 172–174
tax debt, 33
teen driver insurance, 212–213
term life insurance, 221
thermostats, 68
time horizon and risk
  tolerance, 202
Total Accounts section (credit
  report), 139
transportation, ideal household
  budget, 83–84
TransUnion credit bureau, 147

U
umbrella policy program
  liability protection, 212
unsecured lines of credit,
  28–29
utility bills
  fixed bills, 67
  ideal household budget,
    88–89
  money-saving programs, 67
  reducing spending, 67–70

V

vacation budgets, 95–96
Visa, 22

W

wage garnishment, 34
water bills, 68

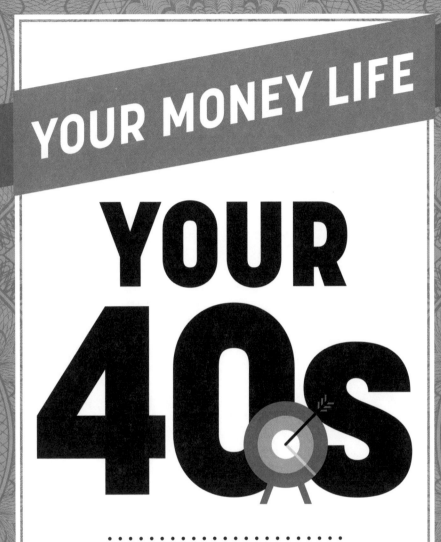

YOUR MONEY LIFE

YOUR 40s

by PETER DUNN

Pete *the* Planner

PETE*the*PLANNER.com

The PATH

Your forties can mean anything from retirement, to buying a first home, to becoming a grandparent, to getting married, to getting divorced, to getting married all over again. All the while, you're heading toward your prime earning years. Your forties is also your last chance to right your ship by choice. If your financial ship is sailing in the wrong direction when you get to your fifties, either you will be forced to change, or you will suffer financially for the remainder of your life.

In a perfect world, this is where you should be by the time you turn 50:

1. House paid off   **2.** Actively cutting expenses   **3.** No longer dependent on your income

Does accomplishing these three goals seem absolutely impossible to you? That's understandable; just know you have some work to do.

Before you make financial changes in your own life, you'll need to deal with the sandwich. No, you don't get a sandwich break just yet. You need to know if you are a part of the sandwich generation, which is made up of your aging parents on one side and your dependent adult children on the other. You could potentially be spending hundreds to thousands of dollars a month supporting others. This isn't sustainable. Your own retirement is just around the corner; if you are misusing your resources on others, your own future is in jeopardy.

DEALING WITH ADULT CHILDREN:

If you experience financial trouble with your young adult children as they get older, their financial struggles are partially a product of your tutelage. Not exactly a fun pill to swallow. Cutting the cord is a two-way street. Your adult children needs to get their financial life together, but you also need to start denying them financial help. Work out how college will get paid for and then cut them loose. Your future is too important to neglect.

DEALING WITH AGING PARENTS:

Whether it's happened already or not, you will eventually switch roles with your parents. This is inevitable and very sad. No one knows how to be retired, which means that no matter how stable your parents' finances seem, there may be cracks under the surface. Maybe they haven't prepared for long-term health costs, or maybe they are spending more than they should. But the reality is, it will become your problem at some point, so identifying the cracks now is important. Have a conversation with your parents. Ask about their retirement. Ask about their estate plan. Ask what your role in it all will be. It will be awkward, but knowing the answers now means you will be prepared for what comes next.

The **PAST**

List your debts, beginning with the debt that has the smallest balance and working your way up to the highest balance debt. Be sure to include all debts; to help jog your memory, see pages 21–37 for a full list of types of debt.

DEBT	BALANCE	MINIMUM PAYMENT	MONTHLY PAYMENT
TOTALS			

The PRESENT  SPENDING

Find money today by working through this list of services you use. Can you decrease your usage? Or switch to a cheaper plan? Decreasing expenses starts here!

EXPENSE	CURRENT PAYMENT	ROOM FOR IMPROVEMENT?	SAVINGS AMOUNT
INTERNET			
CABLE			
HOME PHONE			
CELL PHONE			
MOVIE SUBSCRIPTION			
MUSIC SUBSCRIPTION			
TOTALS			

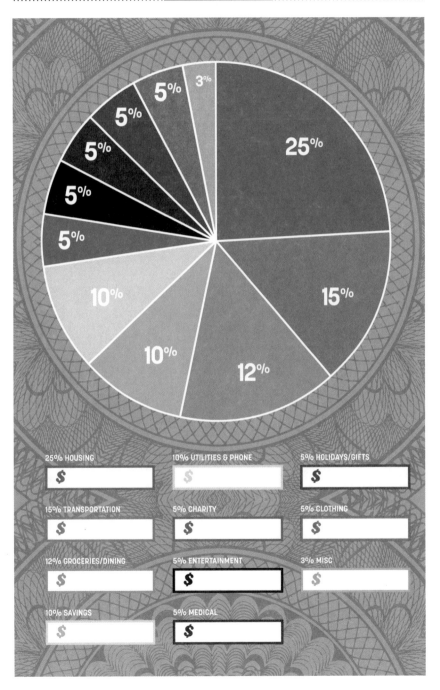

25% HOUSING

$

10% UTILITIES & PHONE

$

5% HOLIDAYS/GIFTS

$

15% TRANSPORTATION

$

5% CHARITY

$

5% CLOTHING

$

12% GROCERIES/DINING

$

5% ENTERTAINMENT

$

3% MISC

$

10% SAVINGS

$

5% MEDICAL

$

The PIE

YOUR MONTHLY HOUSEHOLD INCOME $ _____

HOUSING		TRANSPORTATION	
Mortgage/Rent		Car Payment A	
Electric		Car Payment B	
Gas		Gasoline	
Phone		Maintenance	
Cell		Auto Insurance	
Cable		License Plates	
Internet		Total	
Water			
Waste		**FOOD**	
Lawn Care		Groceries	
HOA		Coffee	
Other		Work Lunch	
Total		Dining Out	
		Total	

BUDGETING CONT.

PERSONAL CARE		EXISTING DEBT	
		(CREDIT CARDS, STUDENT LOANS) NOT CARS	
Clothing		Debt Payment #1	
Cleaning/Laundry		Debt Payment #2	
Hair Care		Debt Payment #3	
Medical		Debt Payment #4	
Books/Subscriptions		Debt Payment #5	
Entertainment		Debt Payment #6	
Gifts		Debt Payment #7	
Pets		Debt Payment #8	
Total		Total	

SAVINGS AND INSURANCE	
Savings	
Life Insurance	
IRA/Roth IRA	
College Savings	
Total	

TOTAL

The POSSESSIONS

In your forties, becoming an expert in the "can I afford it" conversation is paramount to your financial success. Lending institutions of all sorts will trip over themselves to loan you more than you can afford. This means you have to know your own numbers, set your own goals, and follow through with wisdom and restraint.

HOUSE

Current or projected monthly mortgage payment: $

Current monthly income: $

Divide the top number by the bottom number to get the percentage of take-home pay you are spending on housing expenses: $

* 40 PERCENT OR MORE OF HOUSEHOLD INCOME COMMITTED TO HOUSING. Your margin of error is very slim. You are clinically overhoused. You should seek an immediate solution to this problem, especially if you have a car payment, student loan debt, and/or other consumer debt.

* 26 TO 39 PERCENT OF HOUSEHOLD INCOME COMMITTED TO HOUSING. You listened to the bank, or you followed the advice of a mortgage calculator. You are spending too much on housing, but it's not a fatal error. But if you have a car payment or debt, then you are at risk of hating your financial life for a long time.

* 25 PERCENT OF HOUSEHOLD INCOME COMMITTED TO HOUSING. Life is manageable, fruitful, and comfortable when you can limit your house payment to 25 percent of your income. You can get the best of both worlds: a nice home and a nice payment.

* LESS THAN 25 PERCENT OF HOUSEHOLD INCOME COMMITTED TO HOUSING. Do you want everything and are willing to sacrifice a foolish housing decision to get it? Awesome. Then spend less than 25 percent of your household income on a house payment. Travel the world. Dine out. Drive a sweet ride. You can do these things when you don't over-commit to ridiculous housing costs.

Homeowners, also beware of the costly home improvement project! A Home Equity Line of Credit (HELOC) is tempting to tap into, but don't forget, it's debt. The better alternative is to bust your hump and save for the project. Your basement remodel is going to cost $10,000? Cool. *Start saving.*

VEHICLE

HERE'S YOUR VEHICLE SPENDING GUIDE:
What is your net monthly household income? $

What is 15% of your net monthly household income? $

How do your current transportation costs compare to this number? Let's take a look, starting with monthly costs.

Current car payment: $

Current monthly fuel cost: $

Current monthly insurance cost: $

Total monthly costs: $

DON'T FORGET TO FACTOR IN ANNUAL COSTS!

Maintenance: $

Oil-change costs: $

Tires: $

Car washes: $

Repairs: $

Total maintenance: $

Monthly maintenance
(the total above, divided by 12): $

The PICTURE — CREDIT

Your credit report gives you a picture of your financial life. And since pictures are worth a thousand words, let's make sure you know what your picture is saying about your financial life.

Go to **AnnualCreditReport.com** *and use the following table to organize the details from your credit report:*

ITEMS ON REPORT	NOTES
TOTAL ACCOUNTS	
OPEN ACCOUNTS	
CLOSED ACCOUNTS	
DELINQUENT	
DEROGATORY	
BALANCES	
PAYMENTS	
PUBLIC RECORDS	
INQUIRIES	

Trying to improve bad credit? This is how your credit score is calculated. In order to improve your score, work on the areas that get more emphasis in the calculation.

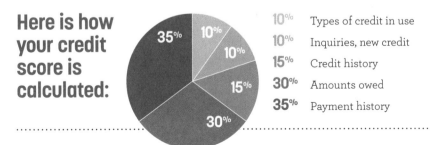

Here is how your credit score is calculated:

10% Types of credit in use
10% Inquiries, new credit
15% Credit history
30% Amounts owed
35% Payment history

The PIGGY BANK

SAVING & INVESTING

WHAT'S IN MY BUCKETS
You have three buckets of money.
Well, you SHOULD have three buckets of money.
It's okay if you don't; we'll help you with that.
These buckets of money will be all you need
to help you along your financial journey.

$

$

$

SHORT-TERM
Bucket #1 is your short-term savings. It consists of three months' worth of your household expenses. When this bucket has three months' worth of expenses, stop putting money in it. If you need money for an emergency, then take the money from this bucket. It is your permanent emergency fund.

MID-TERM
Bucket #2 is your mid-term savings. This consists of down payment money, college funds, and any other amount of money that isn't specifically dedicated to your emergency fund (Bucket #1) or retirement (Bucket #3). You may choose to simply save this money, or you may choose to invest this money. Whatever you choose, make sure you talk to a professional before you take undue risk.

LONG-TERM
Bucket #3 is your long-term savings. You commonly refer to this as your retirement money. Technically speaking, you can't touch this money until you are 59 ½ years old. Is that a ridiculously random age? Yes. Are you in trouble if you don't have any money in Bucket #3? Absolutely. You should start contributing to Bucket #3 as soon as you get a job. Contribute to your retirement account through your employer at least up to what the employer matches.

GO TO **PETETHEPLANNER.COM/RETIREMENT-CALCULATOR**
TO CALCULATE HOW MUCH YOU NEED TO SAVE FOR RETIREMENT.

CALCULATE YOUR NET WORTH

WHAT'S YOUR ASSET TOTAL? $

NET WORTH $

We calculated your total debt earlier. Write that debt total below.

WHAT'S YOUR DEBT TOTAL? $

Subtract the debt from the assets. This is your net worth. It may be positive. It may be negative. Your goal is to make it go in the right direction. You can do this by paying down debt. You can do this by saving money. Or you can do this by doing both. *Do both.*

The PITFALLS

*Keep yourself organized by charting
your insurance coverage here:*

TYPE OF INSURANCE	COVERAGE IMPROVEMENT?	MONTHLY PREMIUM	ROOM FOR IMPROVEMENT?
HEALTH			
CAR			
RENTERS			
HOMEOWNERS			
LIFE			
DISABILITY			

THE PLAN

Your forties is the hardest decade of all. Each decade of a person's life presents challenges, but there's something ominous about your forties. If you leave your forties with significant financial struggles, there is very little recourse for your future. If you hit 50 and you are still mired in overspending, debt, and an empty retirement account, you're in serious trouble. You must take action now.

AS YOU WORK YOUR WAY UP TO AGE 50, FOCUS ON ACCOMPLISHING THESE GOALS:

- Establish and contribute to a college fund for your kids, and/or pay off Parent PLUS Loans.
- Pay off your own student loans.
- Each year, increase your contribution percentage to your retirement fund and work toward contributing up to the government cap.
- Begin a relationship with a good financial advisor.
- Avoid making new debt commitments.
- Save at least 20% of your income.
- Pay off your home, or at the very least make a plan to have your home paid off pre-retirement.

Need an extreme solution? Good for you. Going the extreme solution route isn't easy, but it's the best way to get back on the right track.

1. GET AN ADDITIONAL JOB
Once you've exhausted your opportunities to decrease your spending, earning more income can be a solution. If you get an additional job and bring in more income but haven't decreased your spending, then you'll have only created a bigger problem. Doing so before getting a second job will ensure you know exactly how much extra you need to make in order to reach your financial goals. Do you need $500 a month in order to pay off debt or save for college? Okay, go out and find a job that can help you reach that goal. Also, give yourself a deadline. A second job is never going to be appealing, but if you give yourself a timeline to complete your goal, then working extra for a six-month period will be more palatable.

2. SELL YOUR HOUSE
Housing decisions can break you, and maybe you already know this firsthand. Your home is not only your largest expense, but often your largest emotional anchor. Be honest with yourself; is your emotional anchor causing major financial stress and disruption to your life? If so, it's time to consider selling. You wanted an extreme solution, and this is one, but it's also one that could bring the greatest amount of freedom to your financial life.